This Book Belongs To:

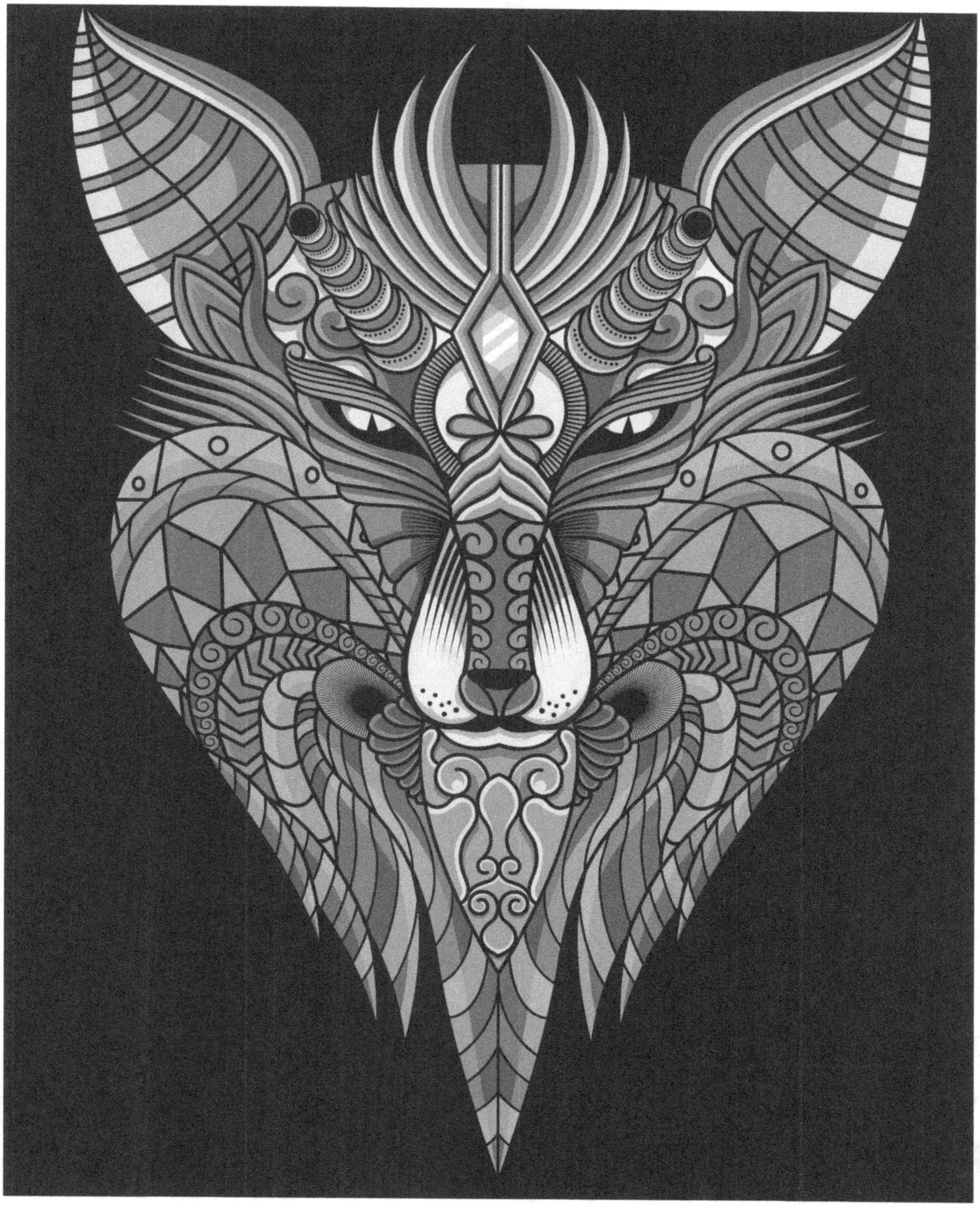

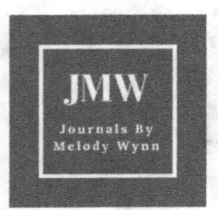

COLOR TEST

TEST YOUR COLOR SUPPLIES ON THIS PAGE TO SEE HOW THEY REACT TO THE PAPER. PLACE A BLANK PAGE OR TWO BEHIND EACH PAGE AS YOU COLOR, TO PREVENT COLORS FROM BLEEDING THROUGH TO THE NEXT PAGE.

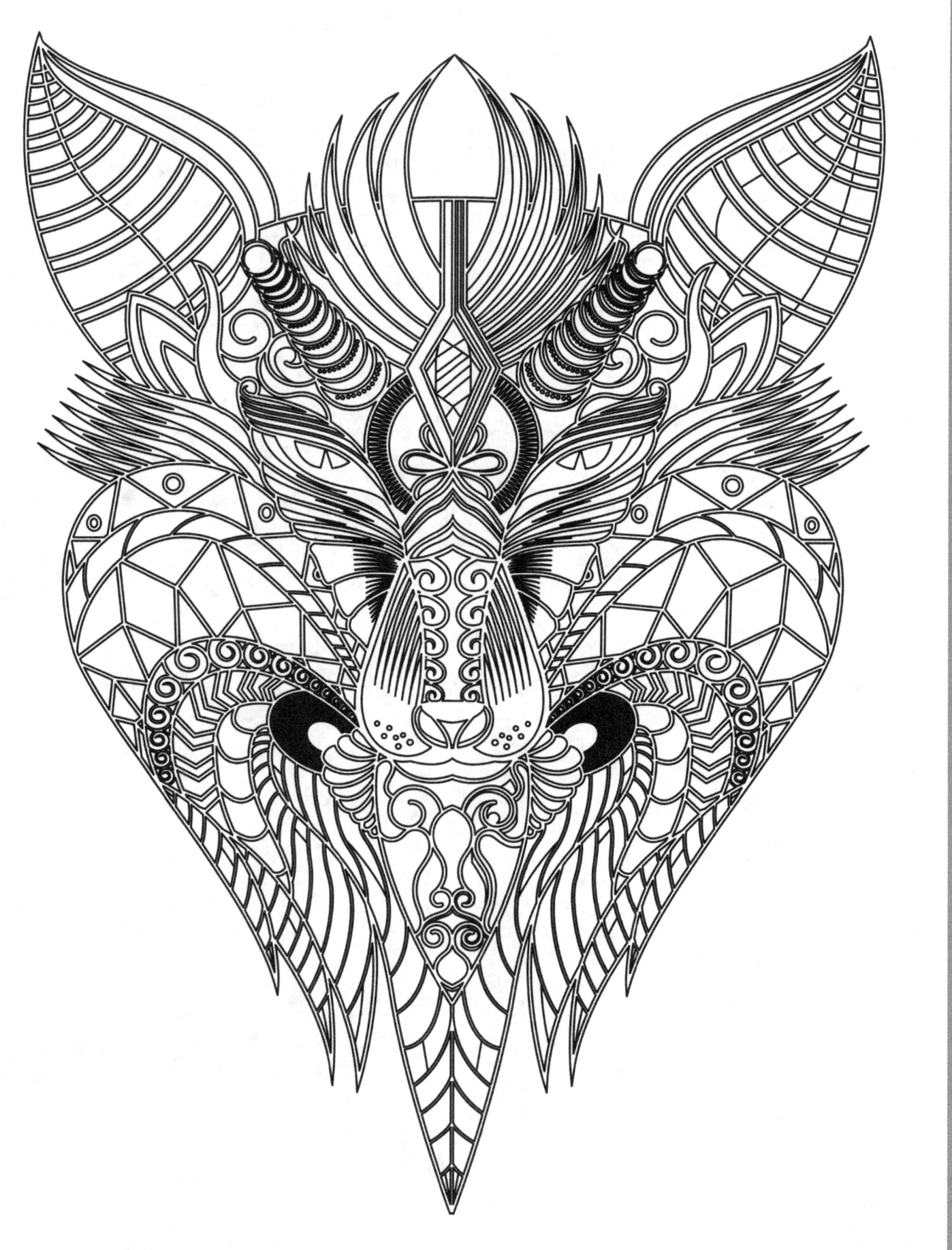

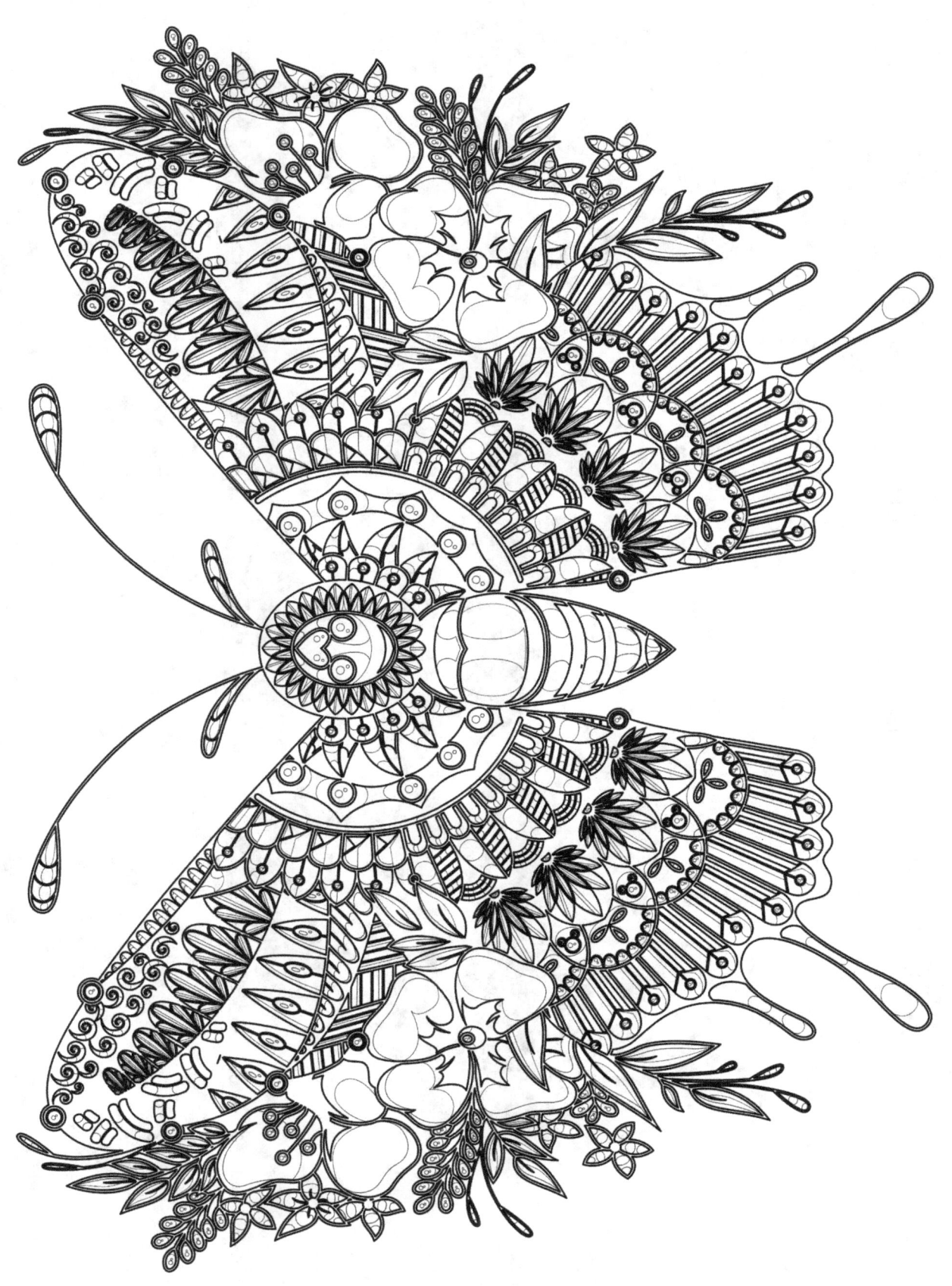

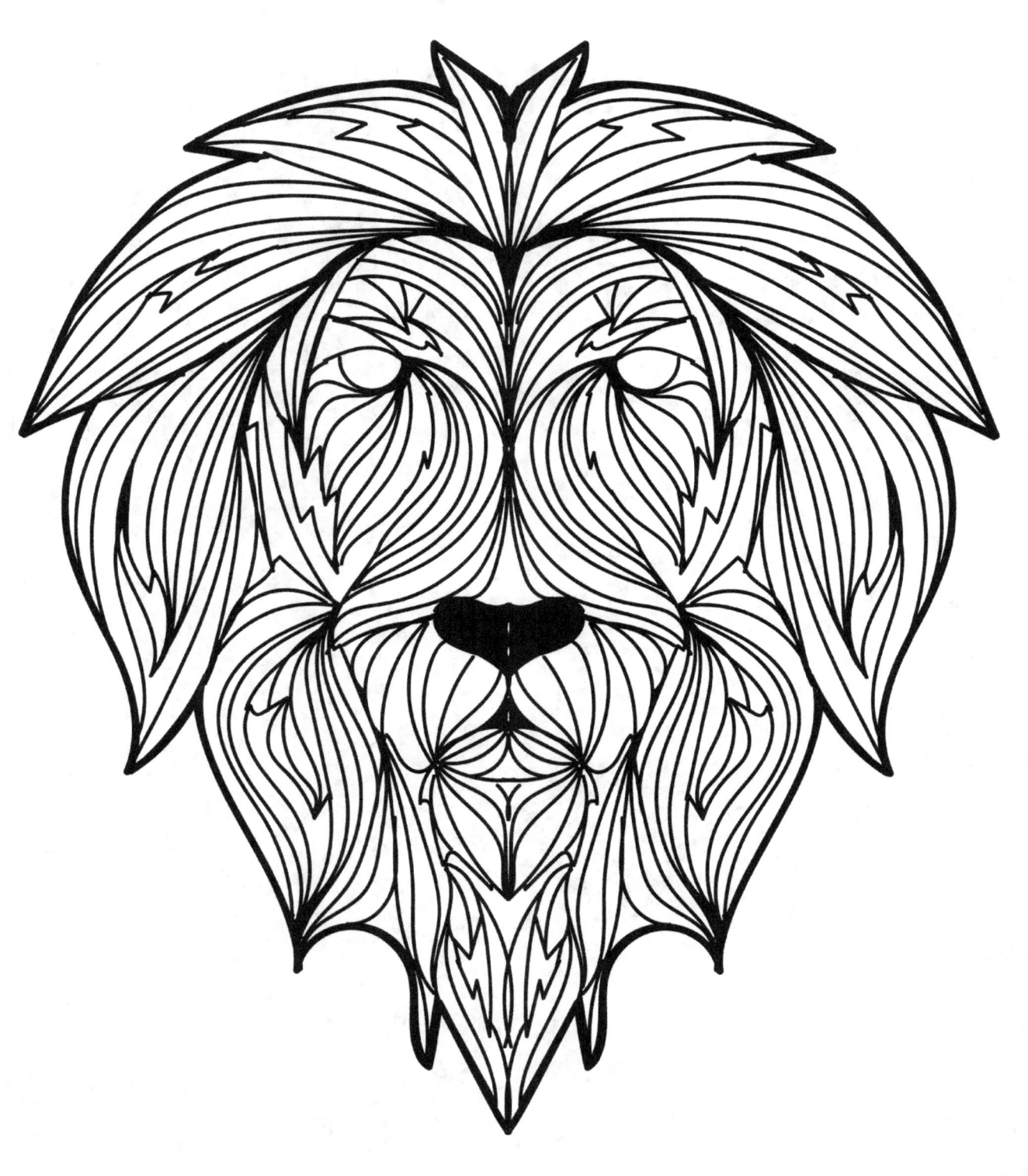

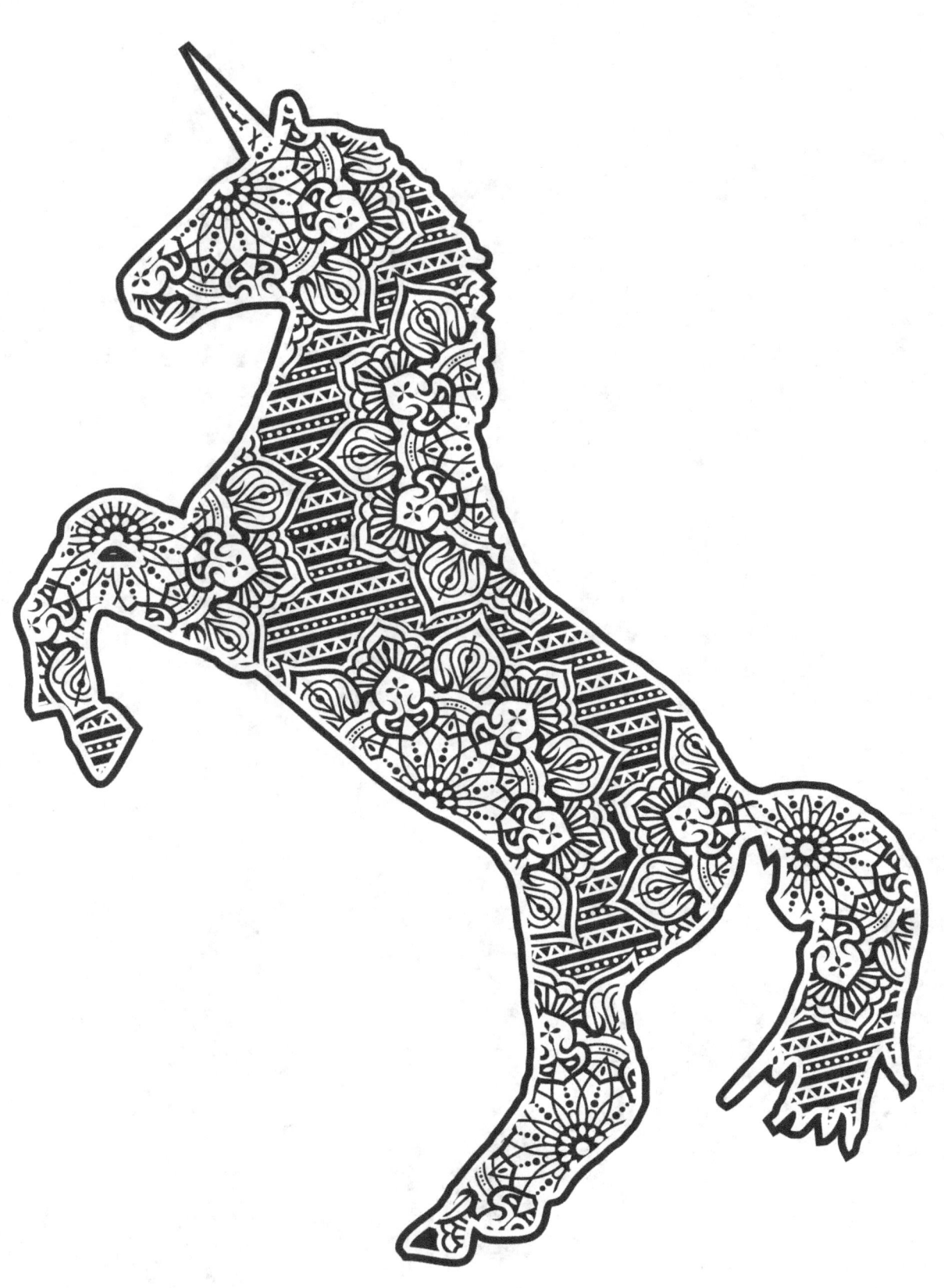

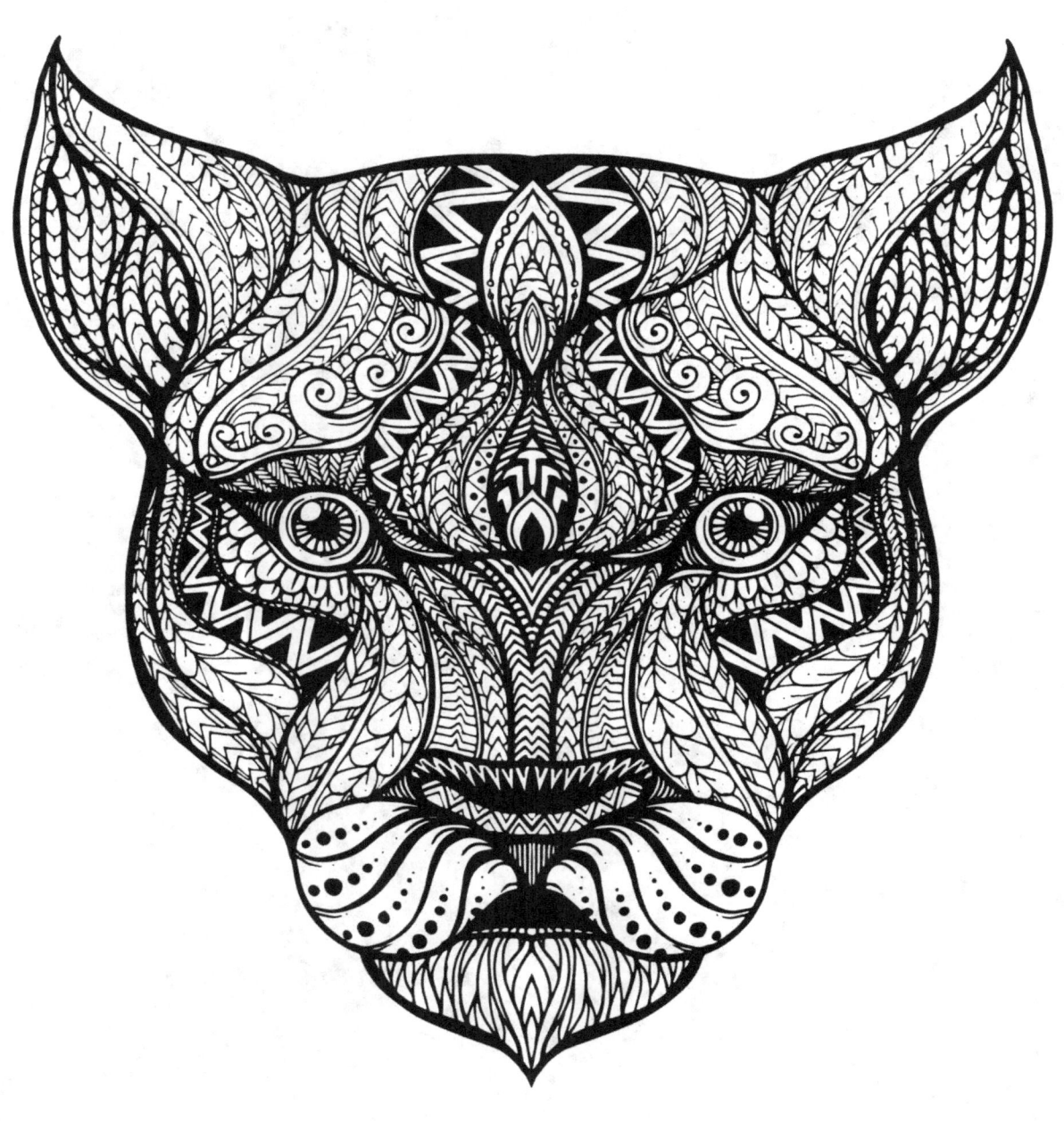

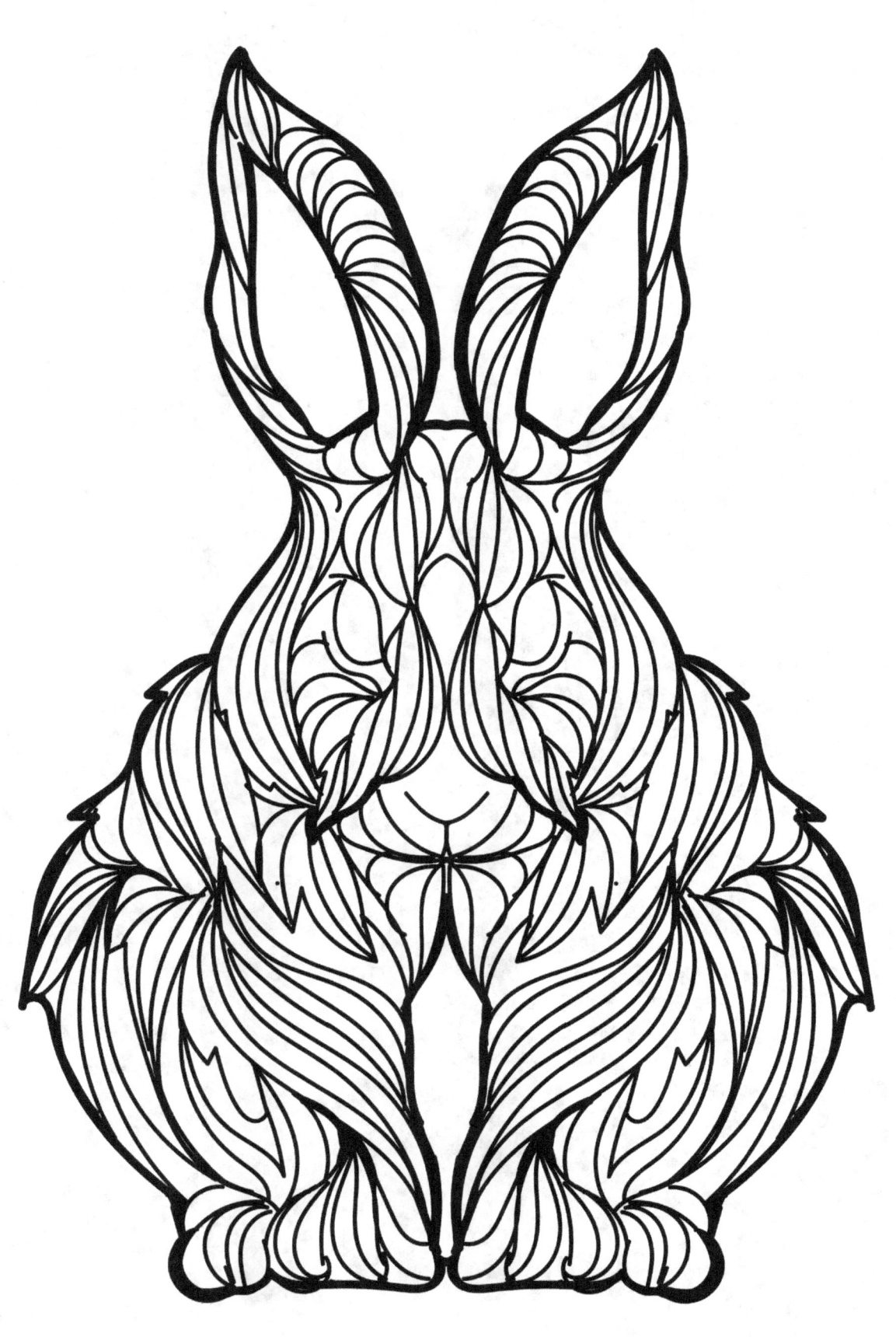

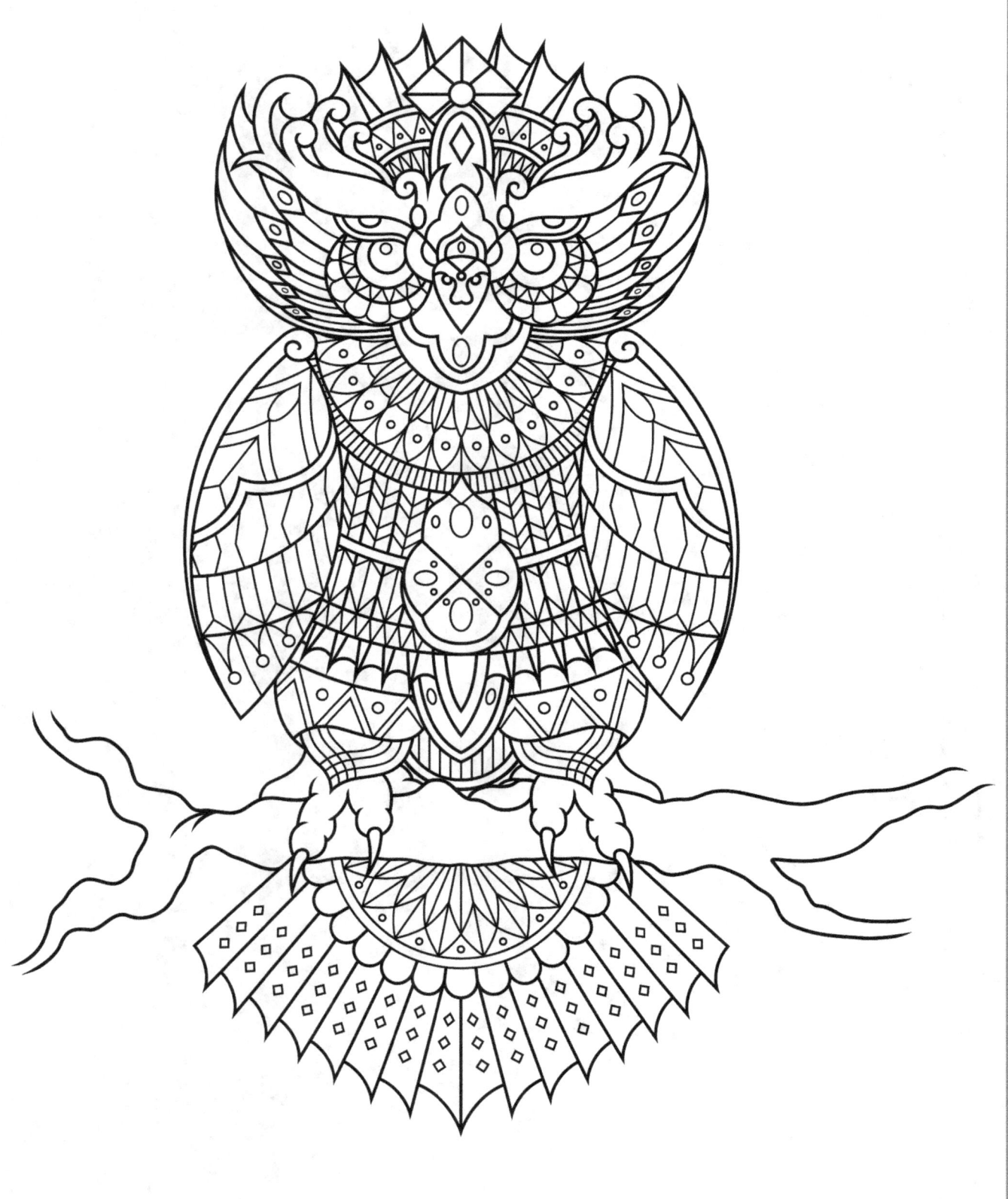

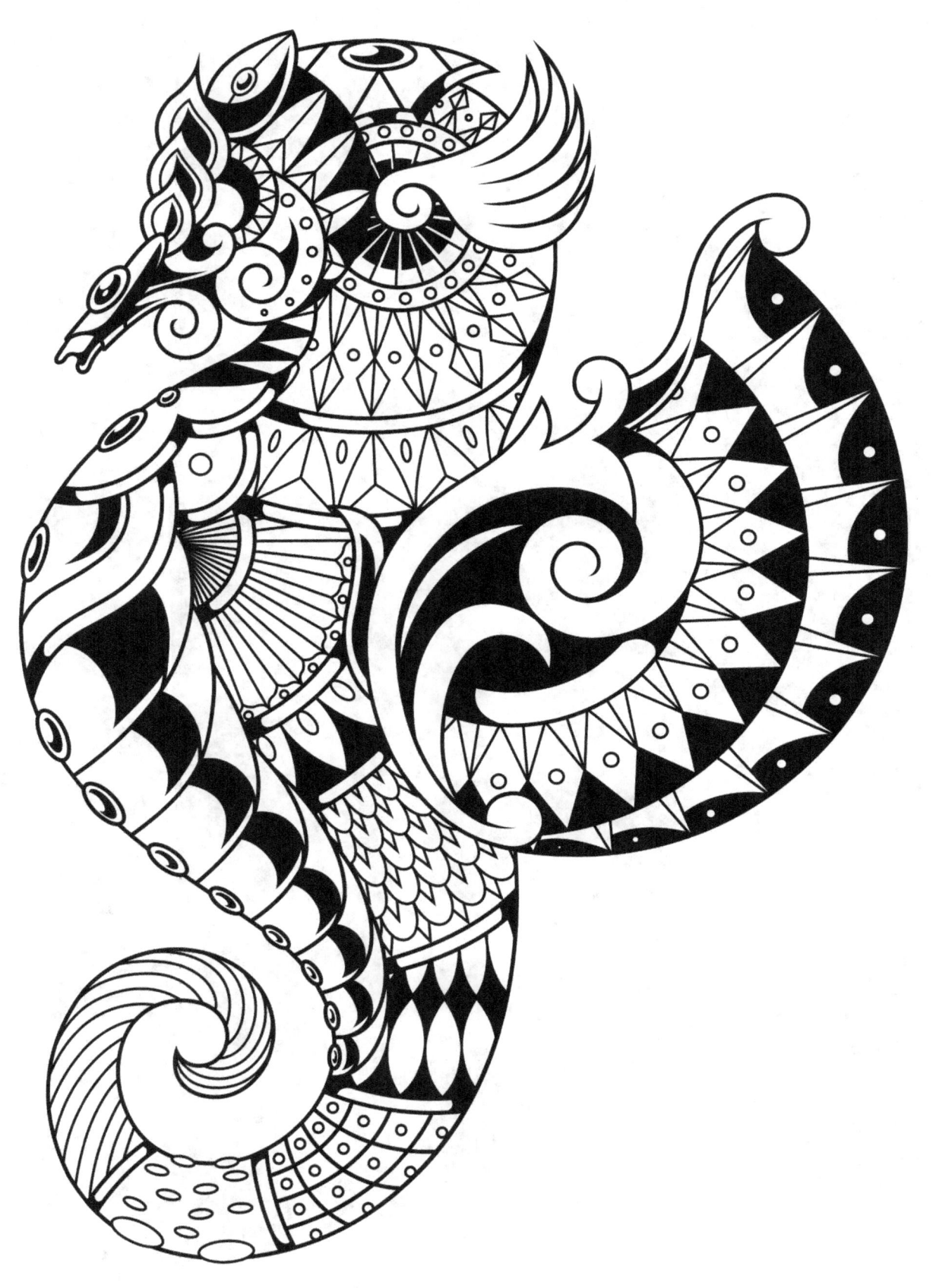

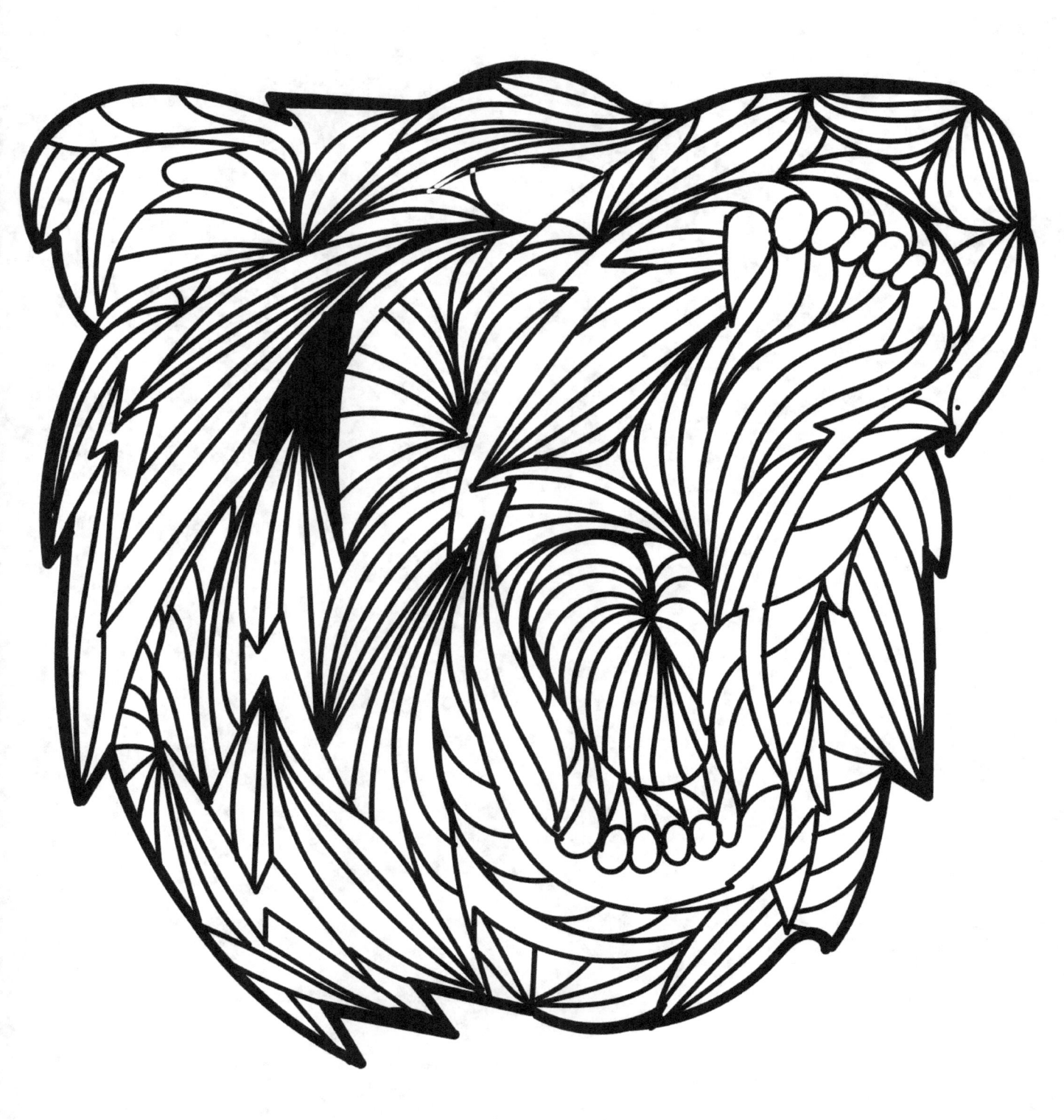

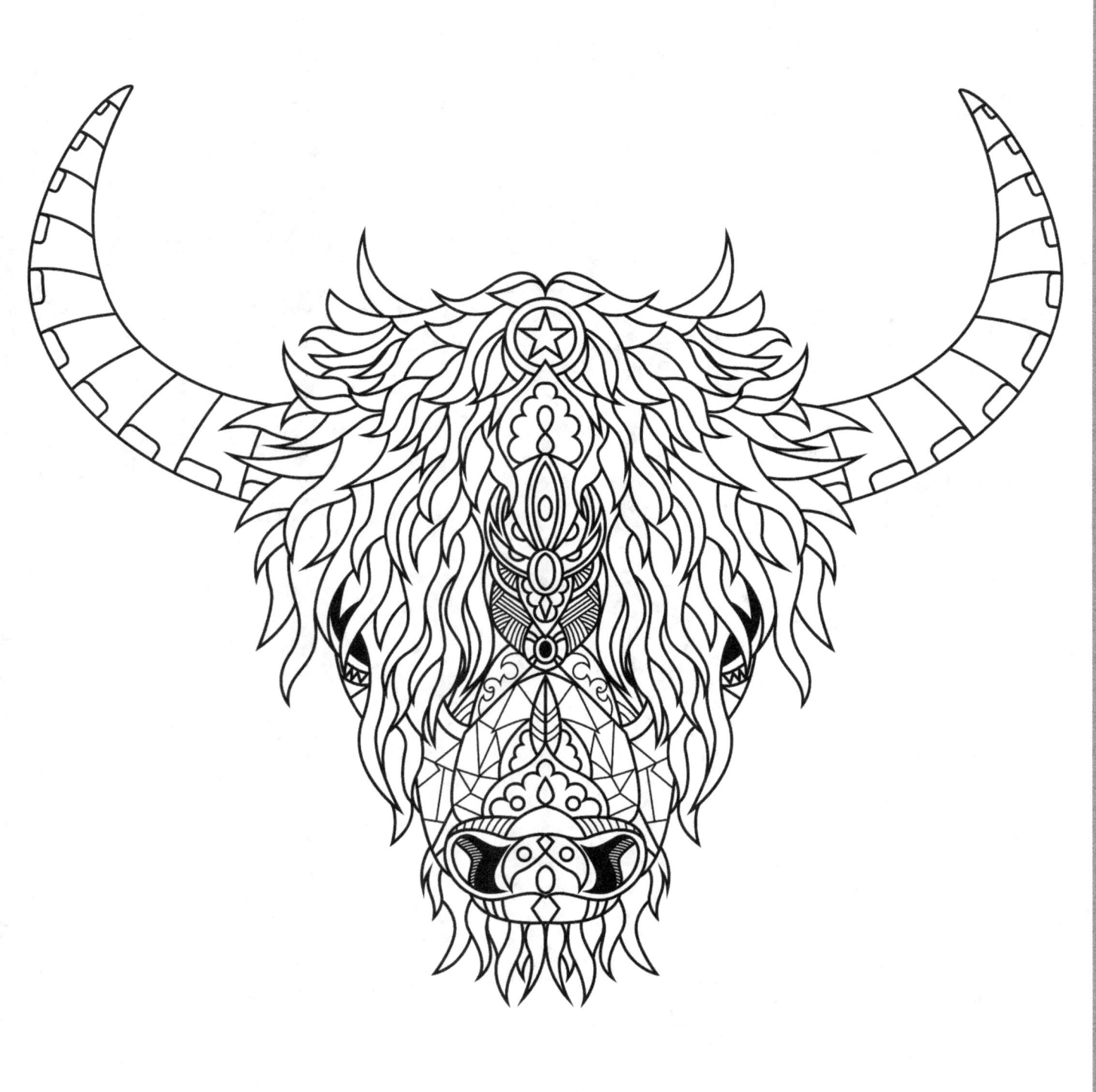

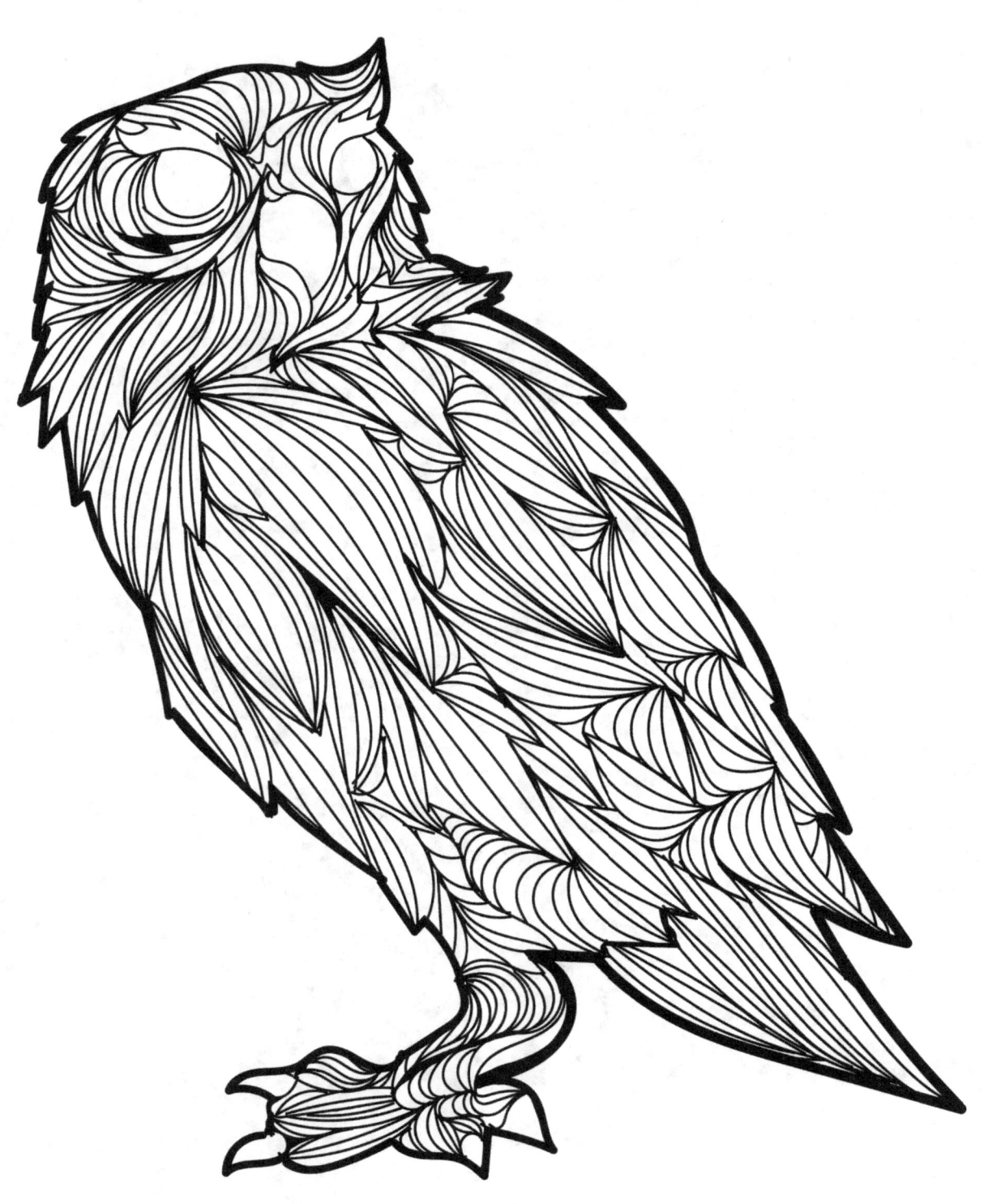

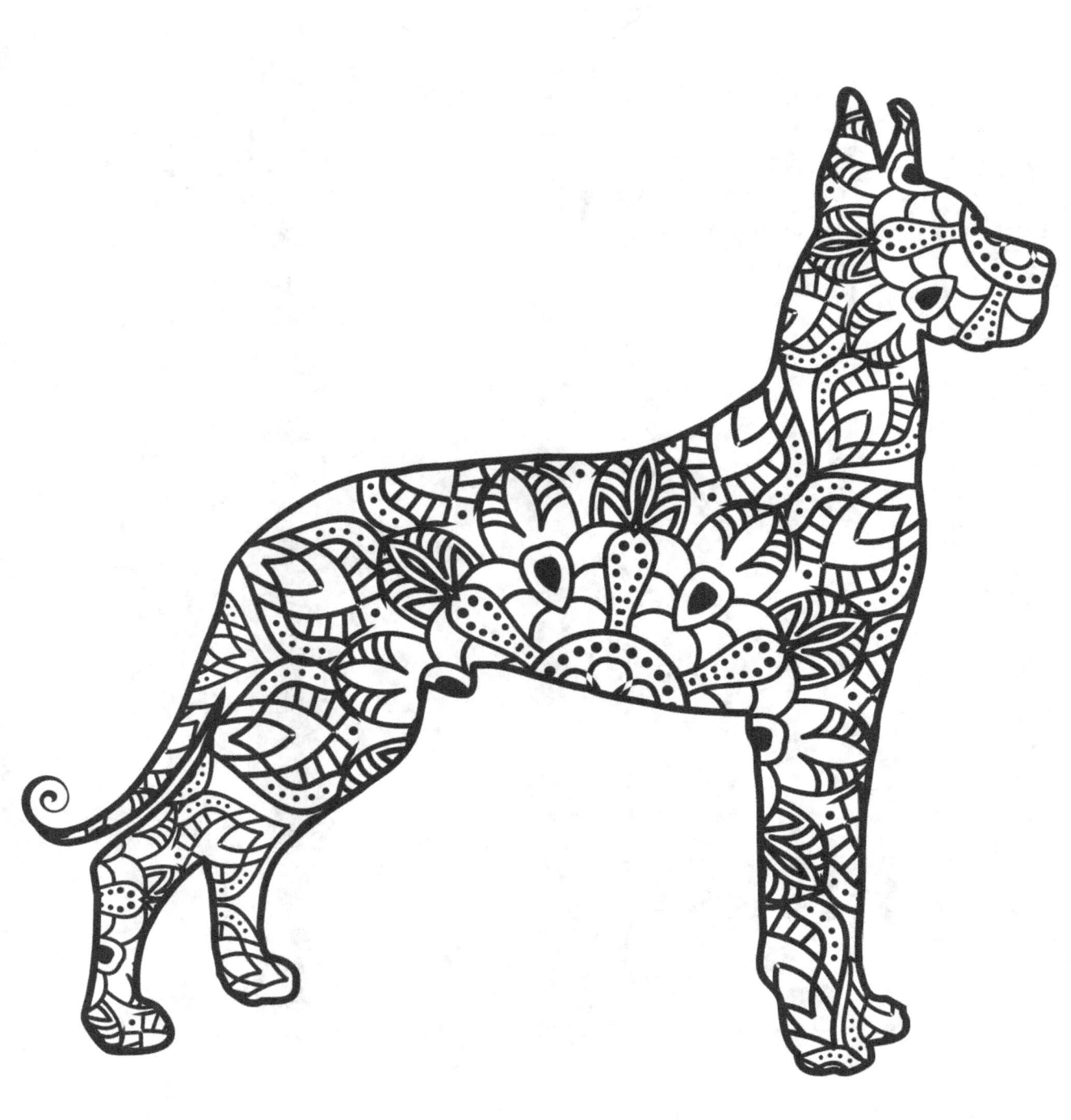

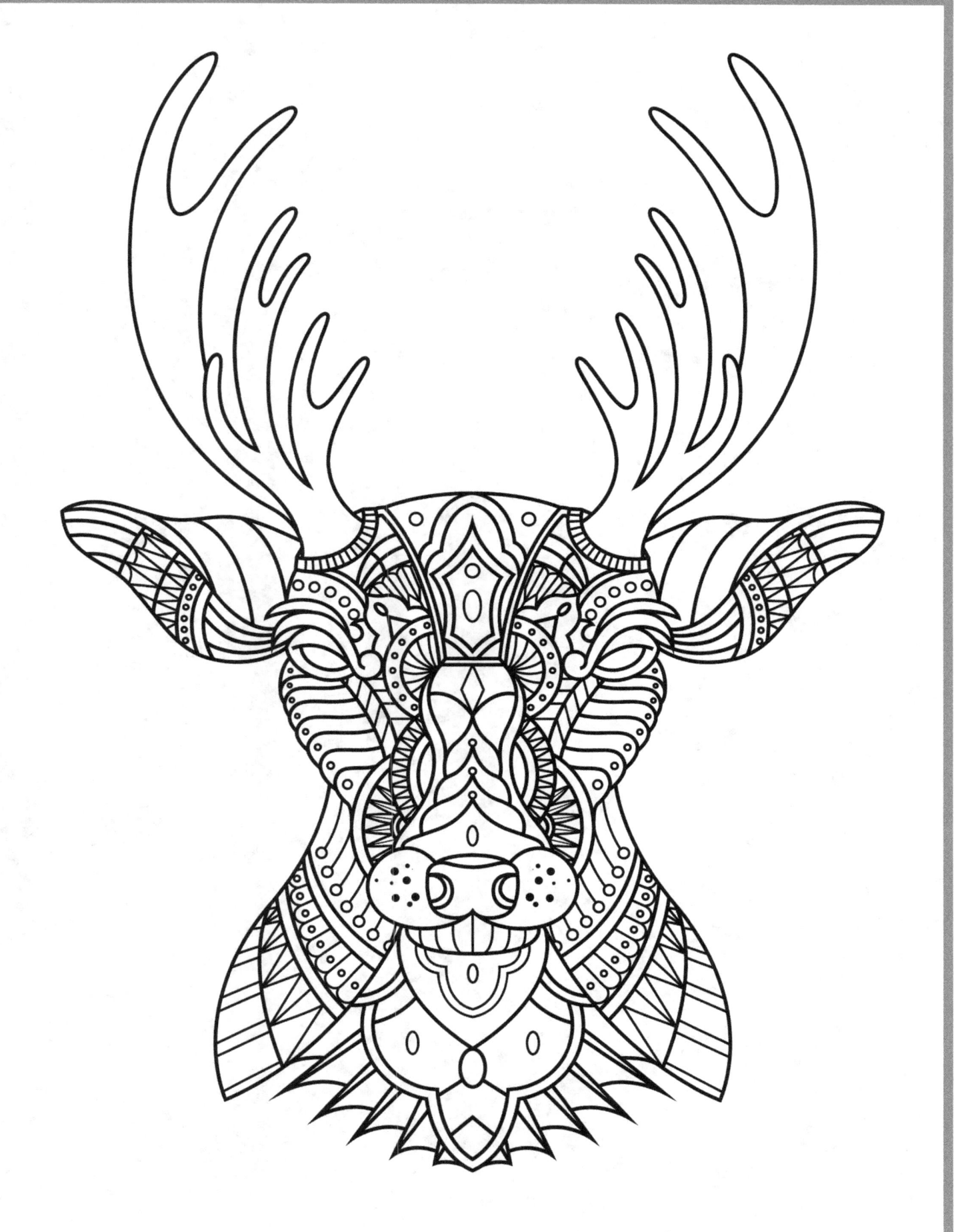

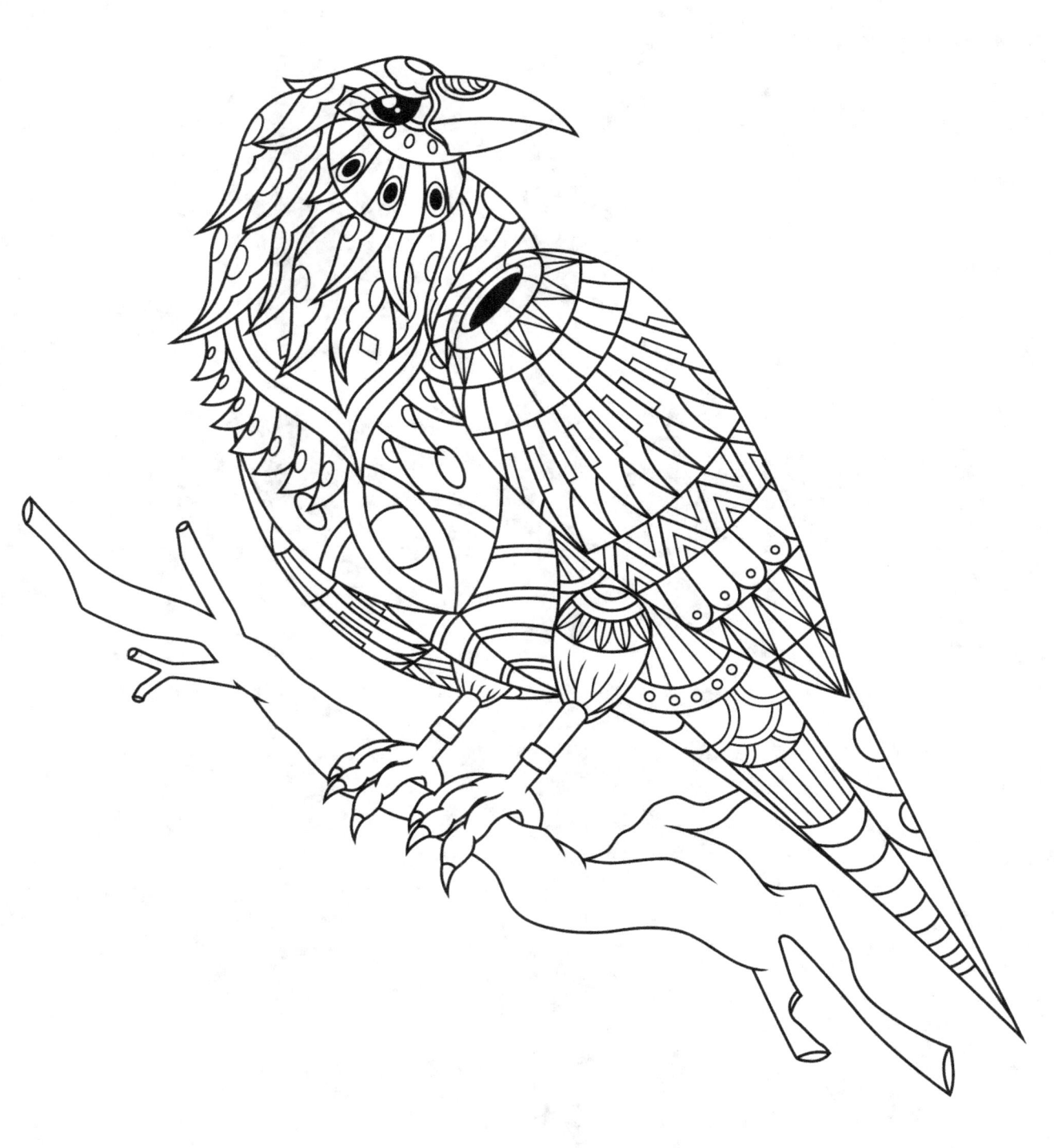

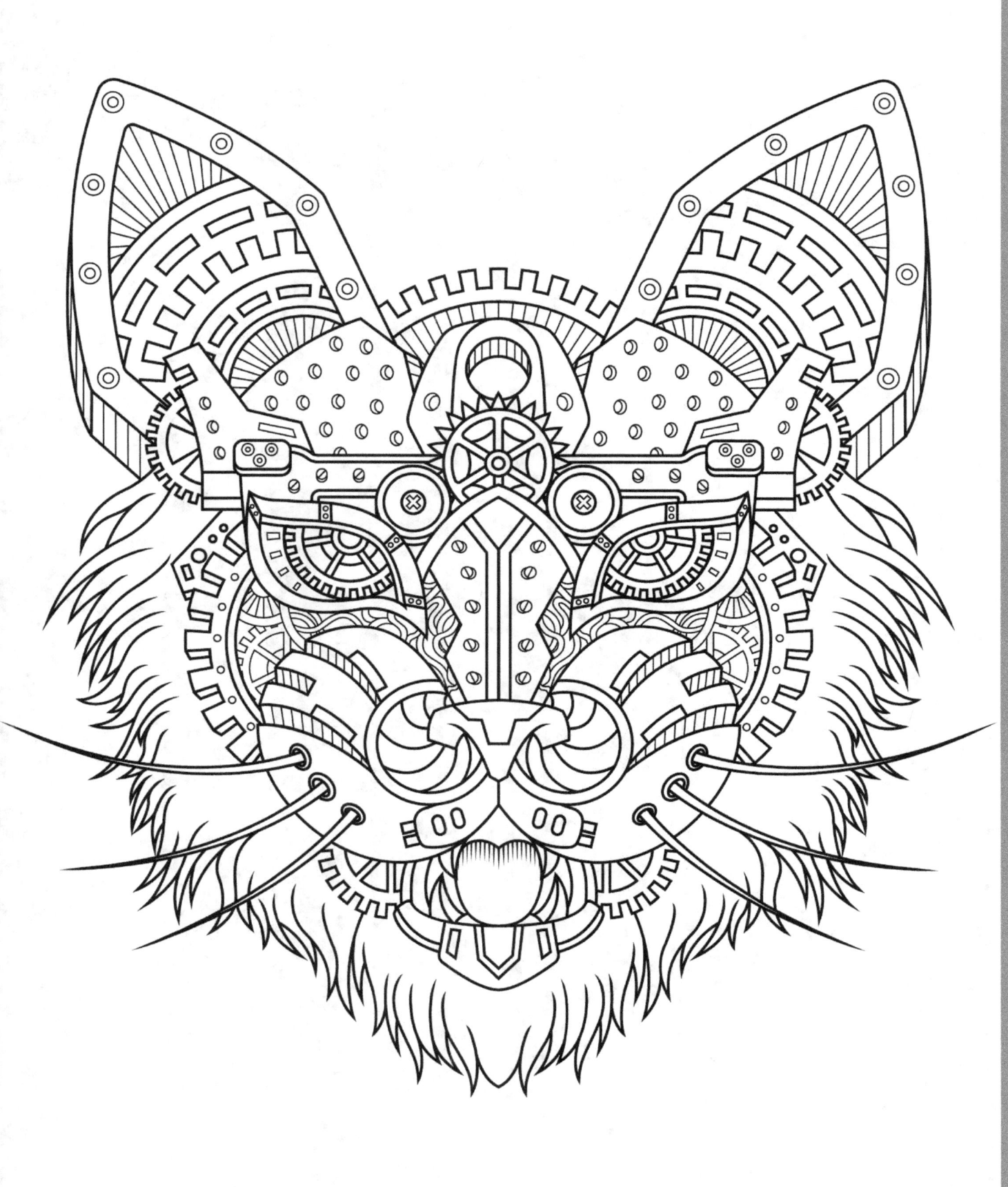

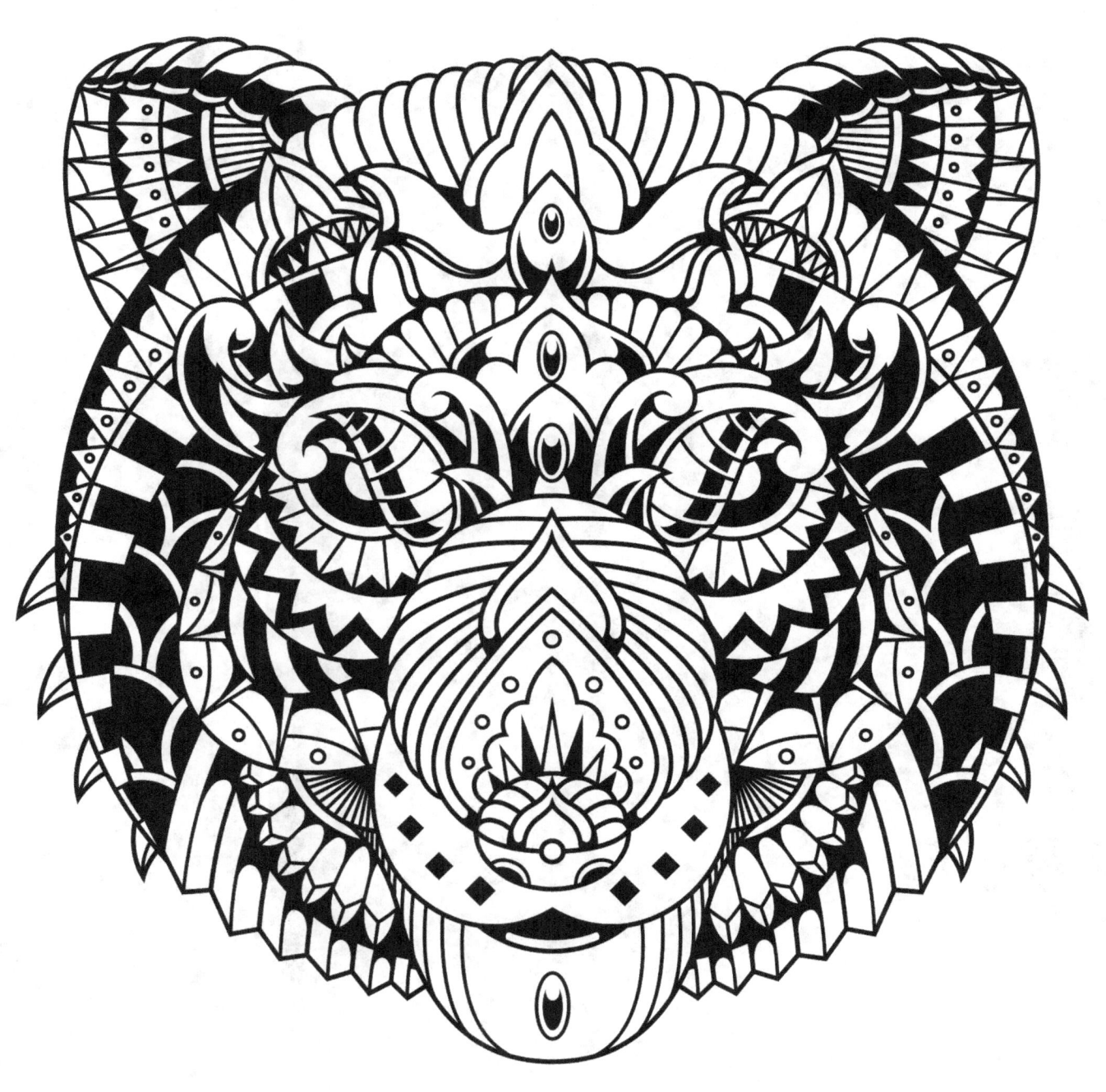

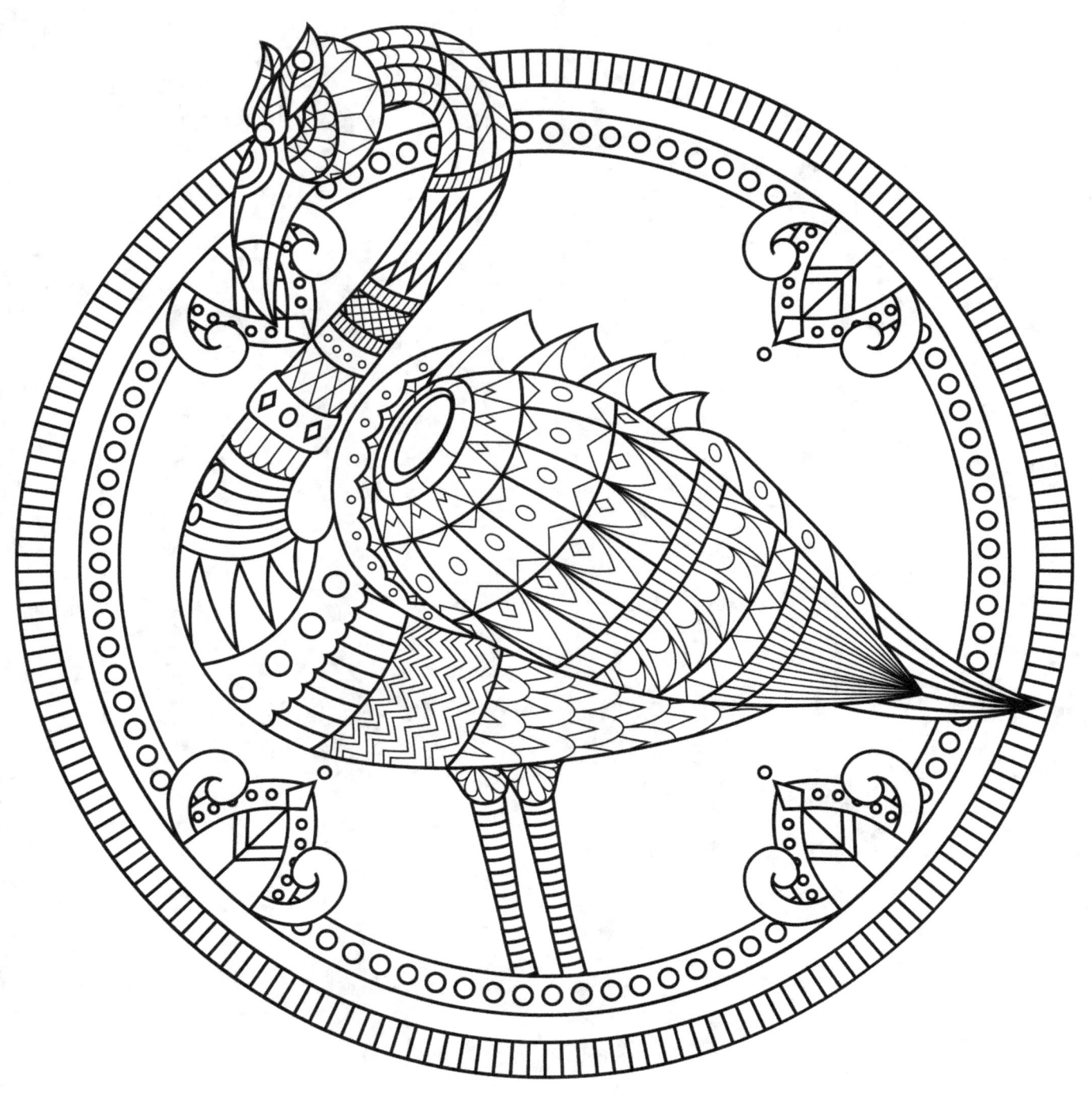

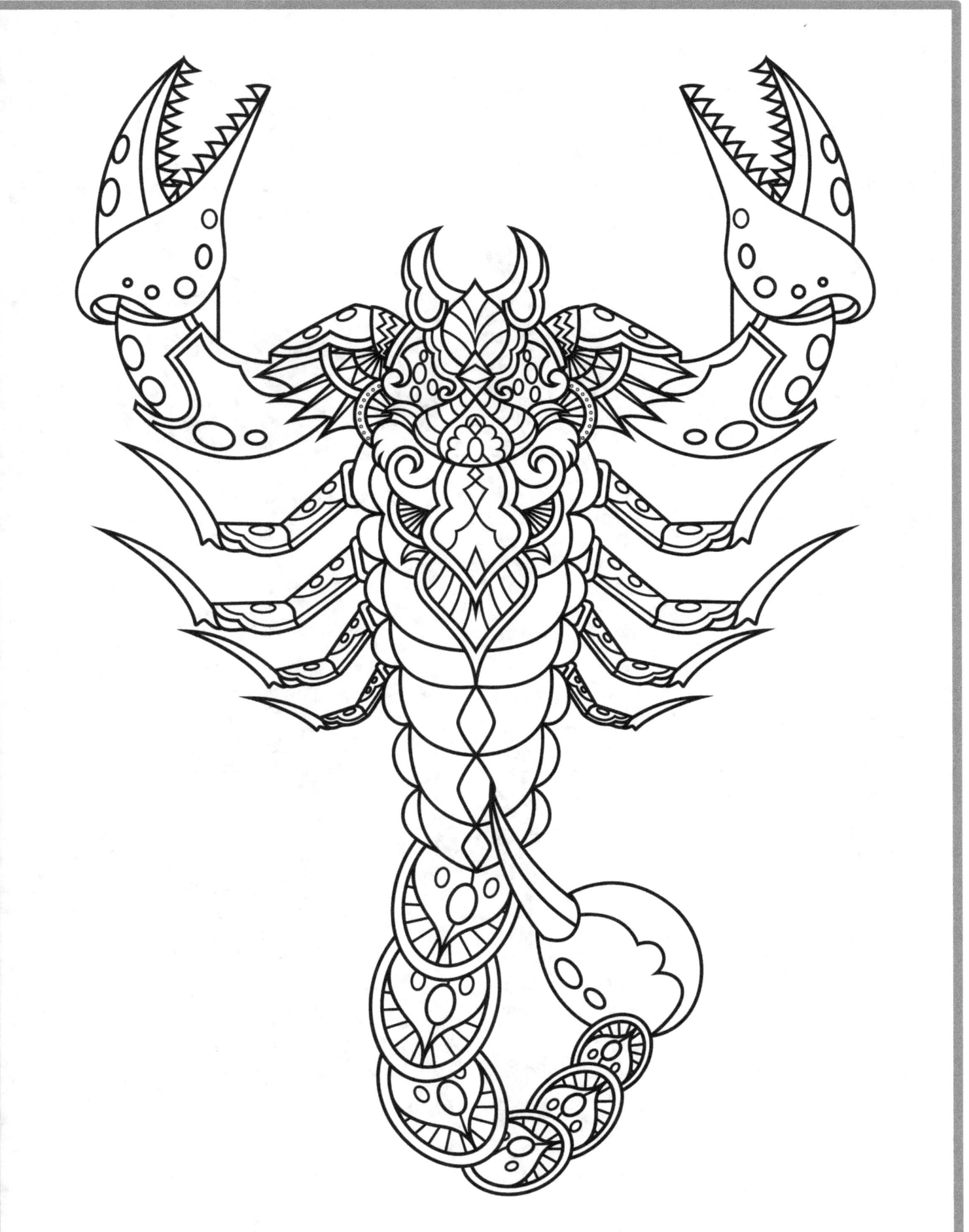

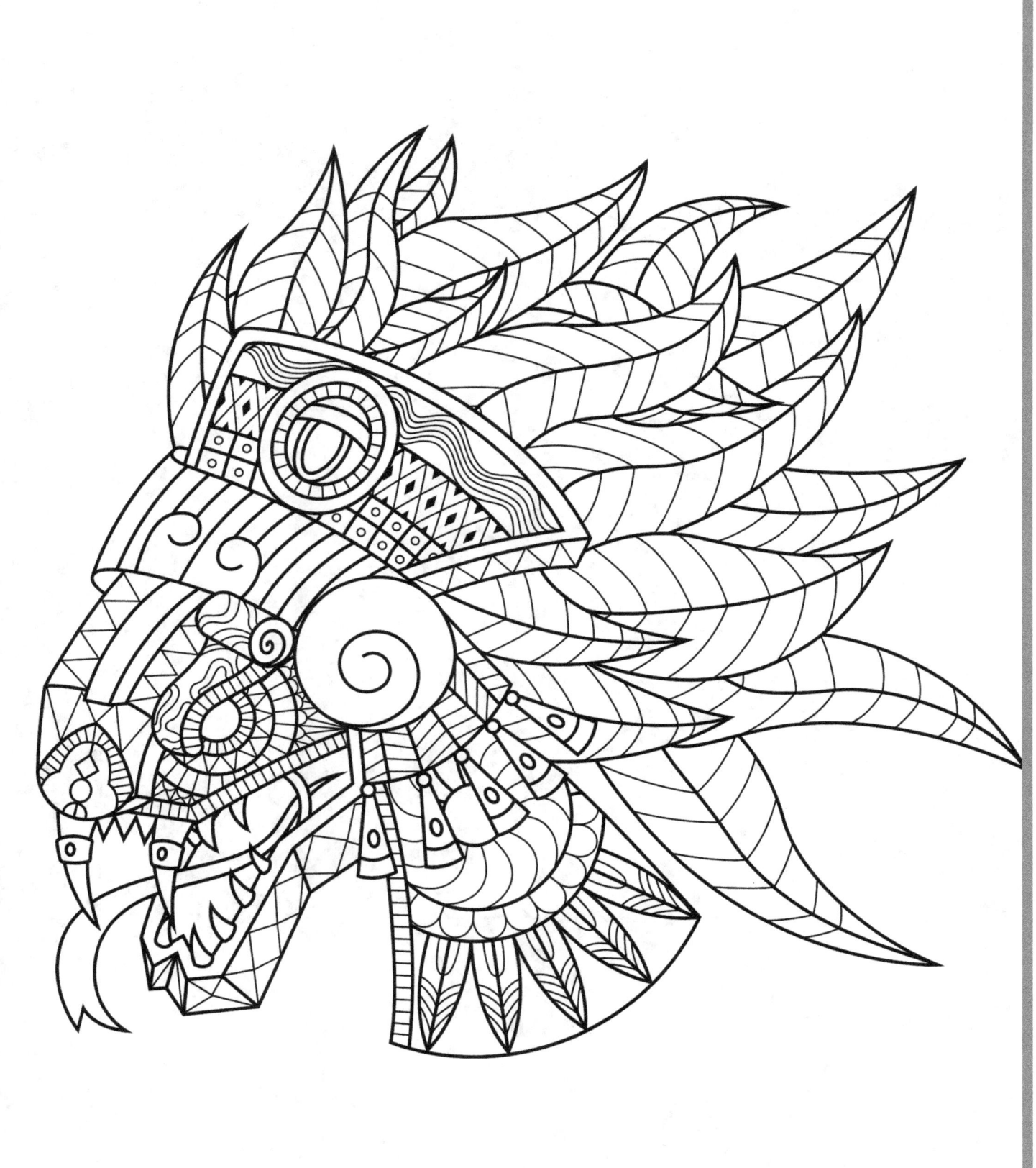

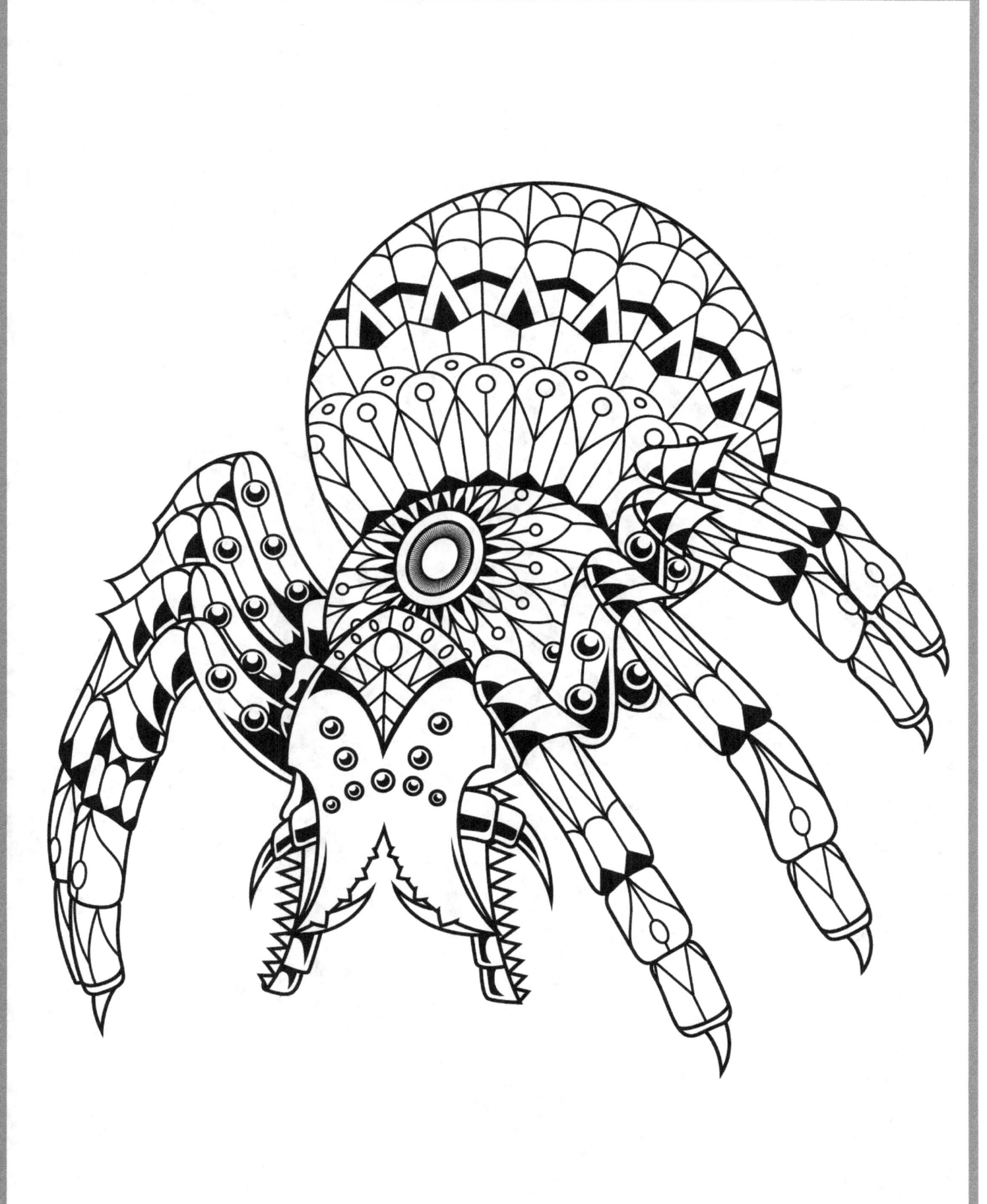

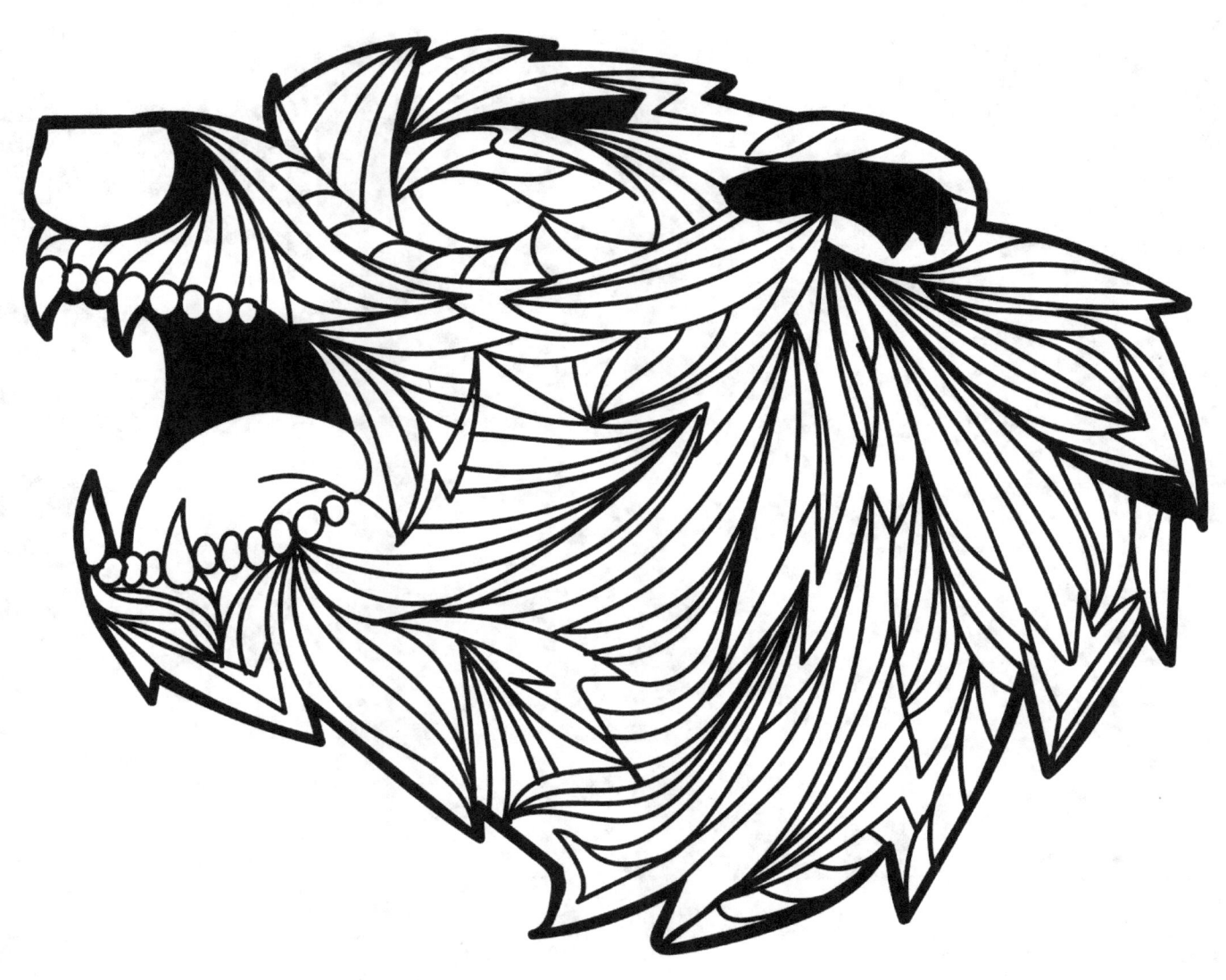

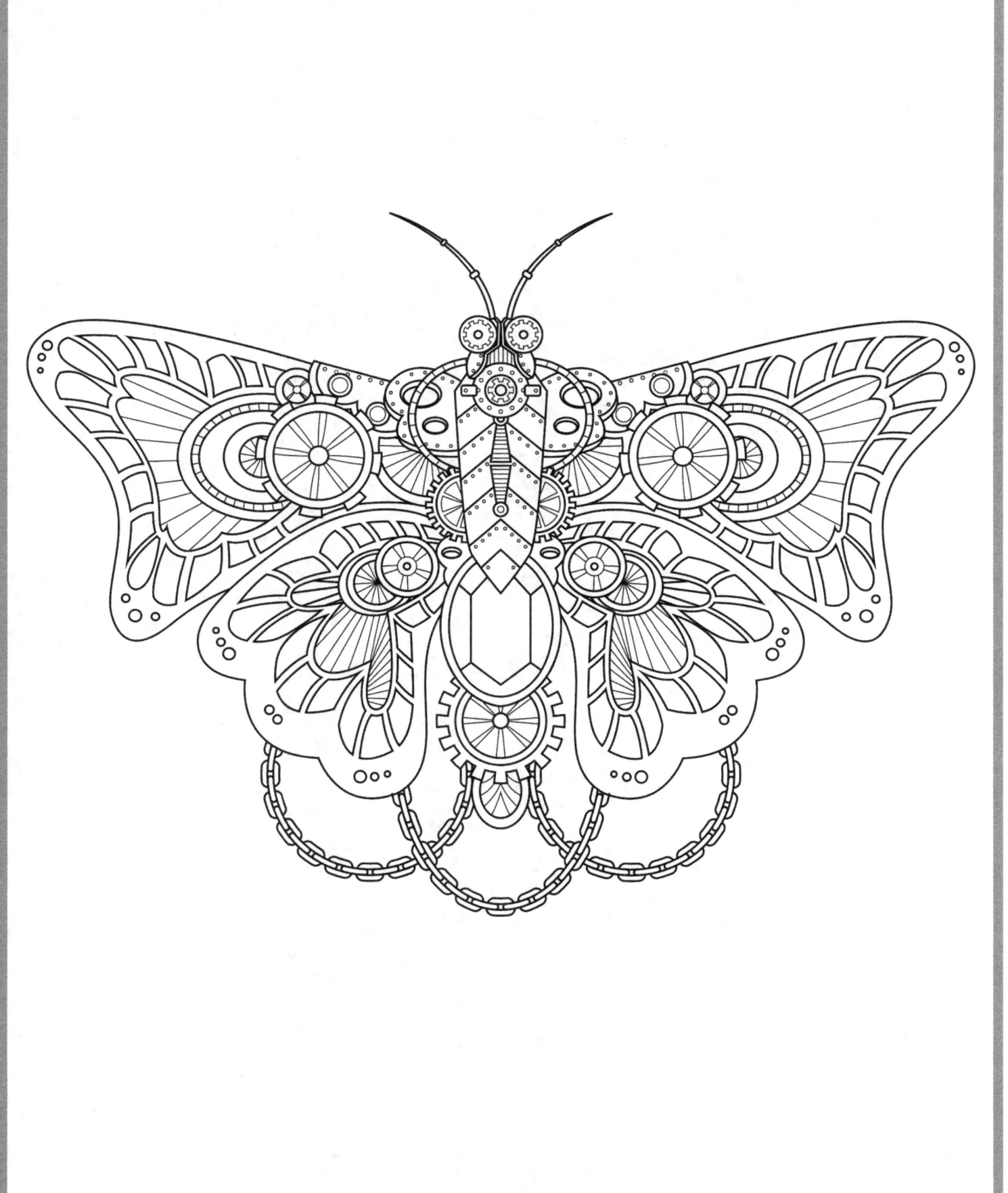

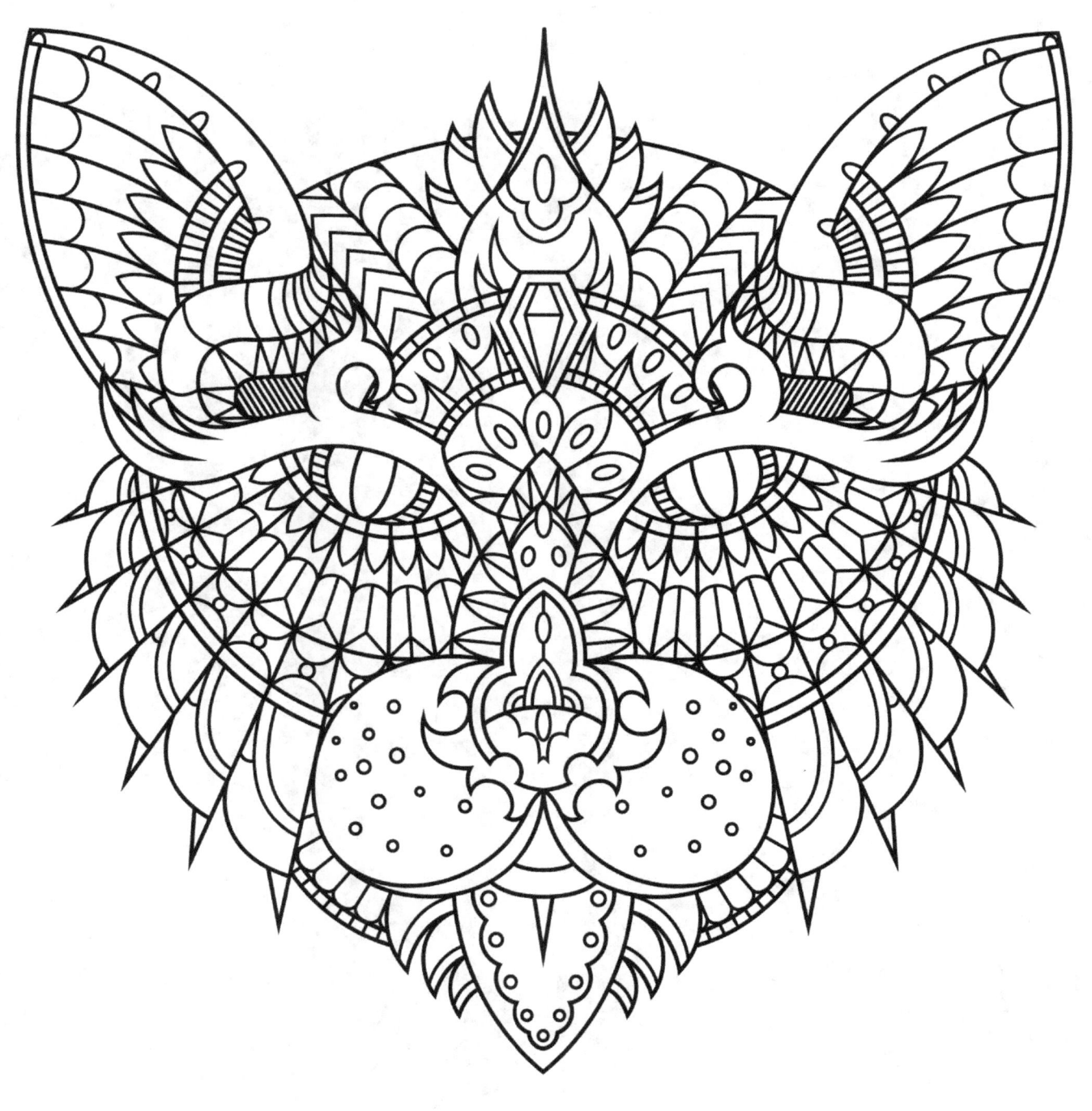

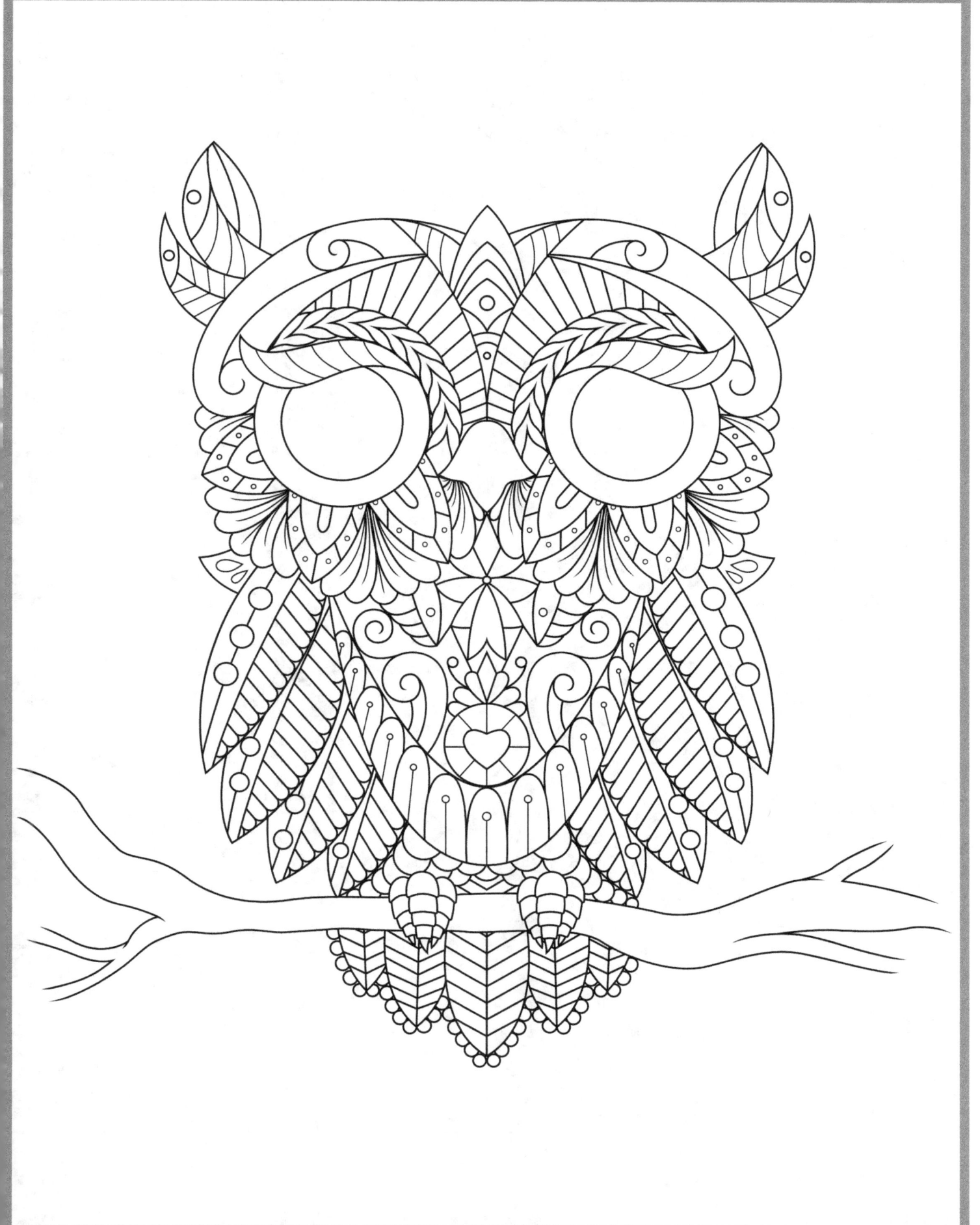

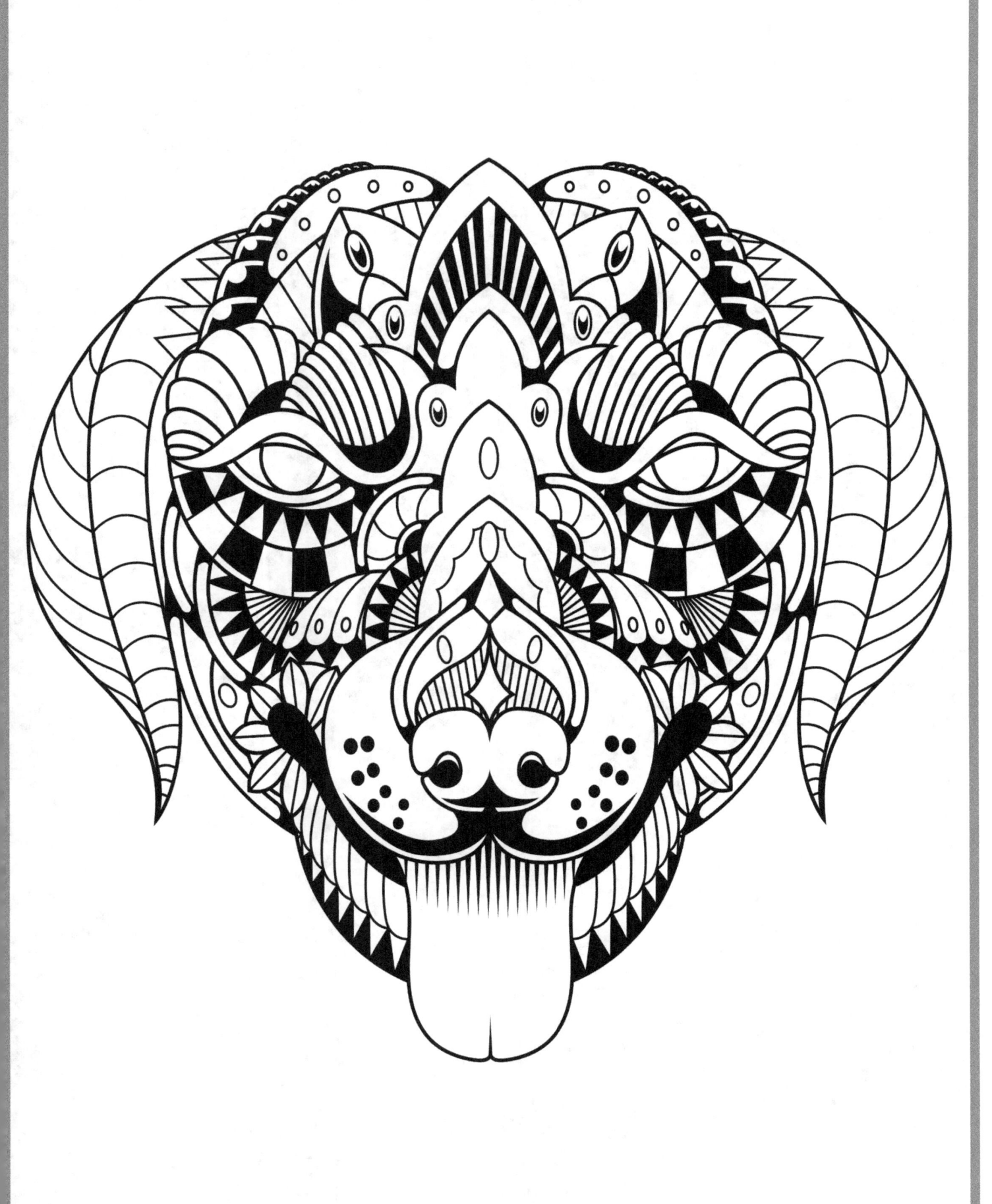

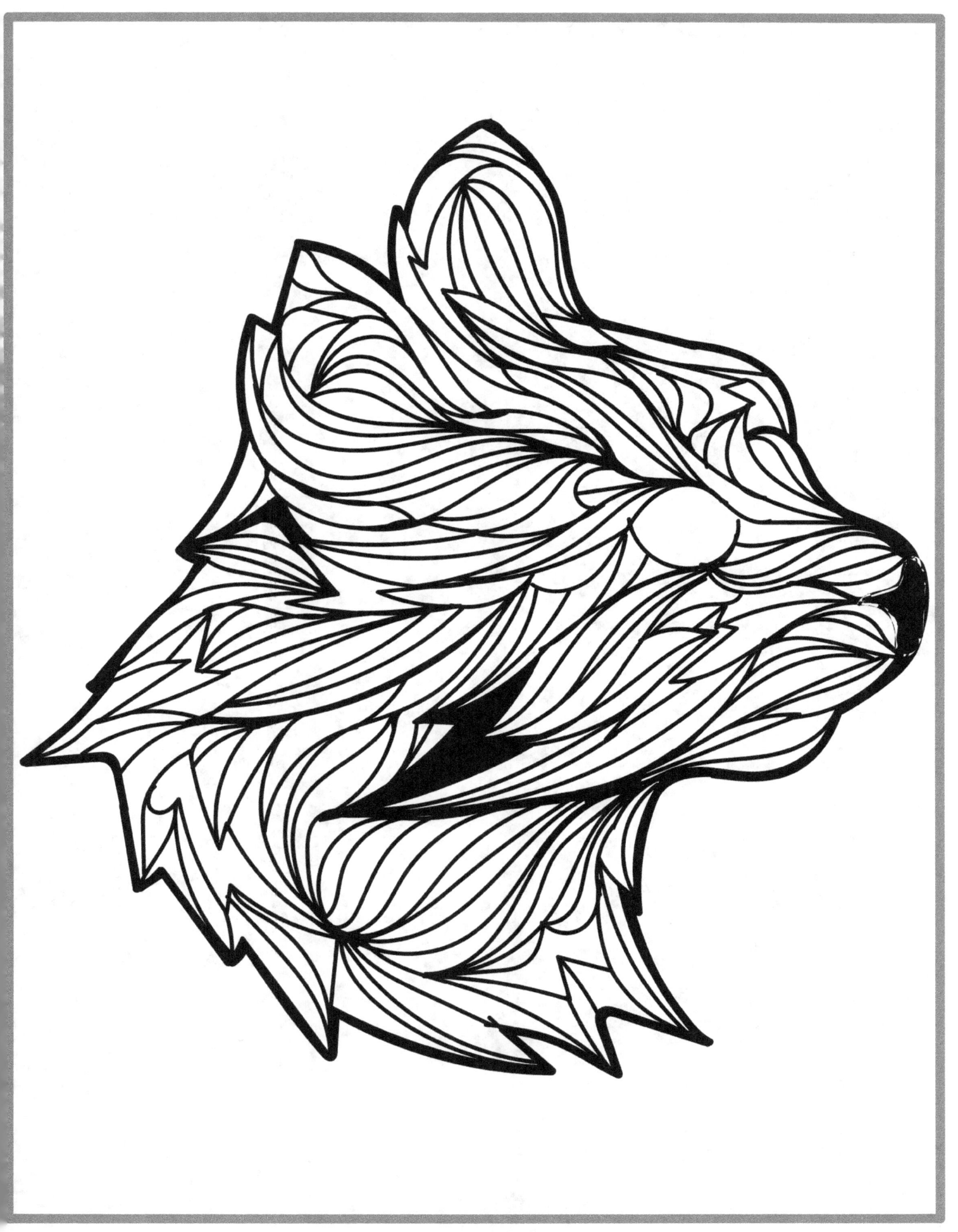

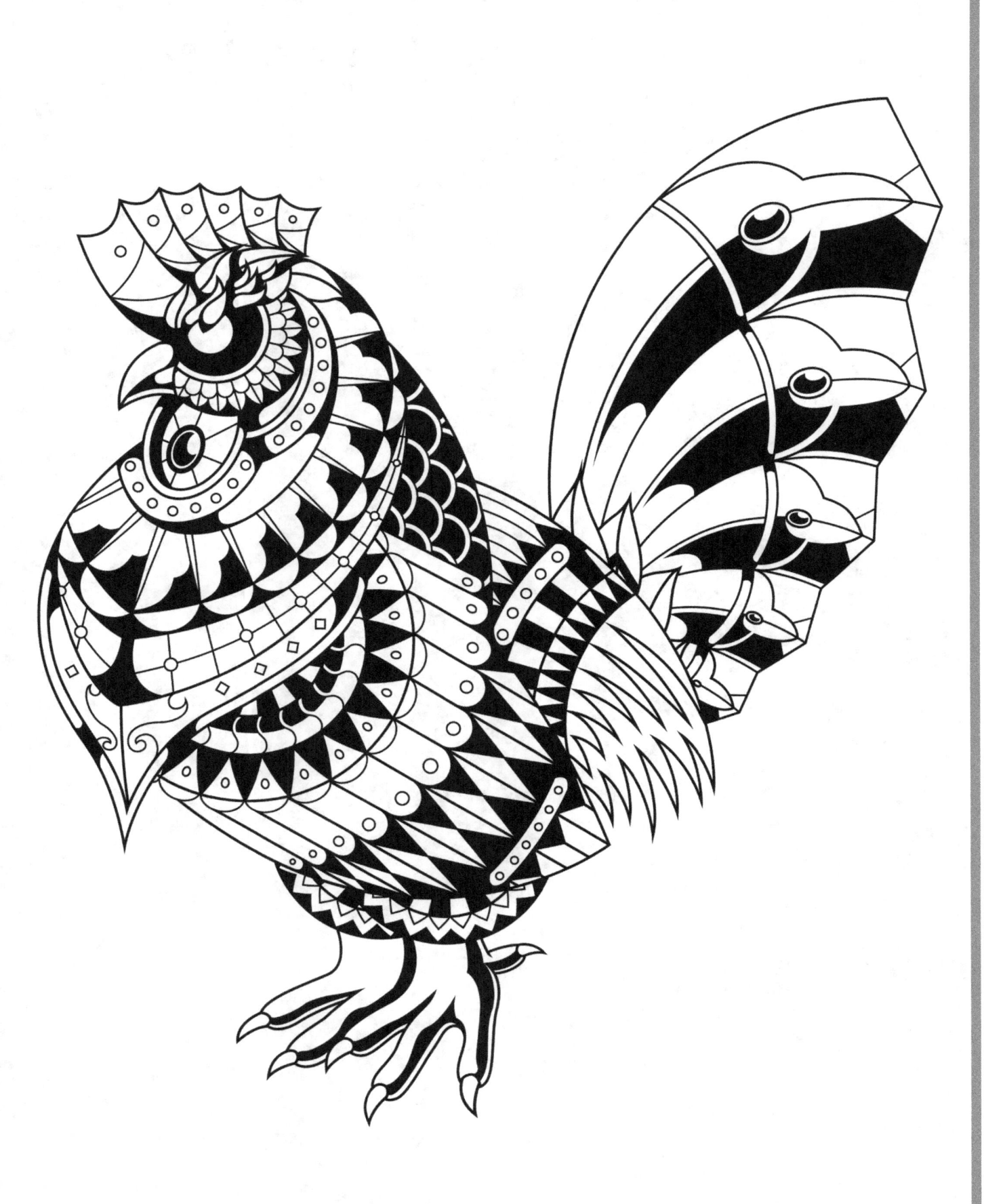

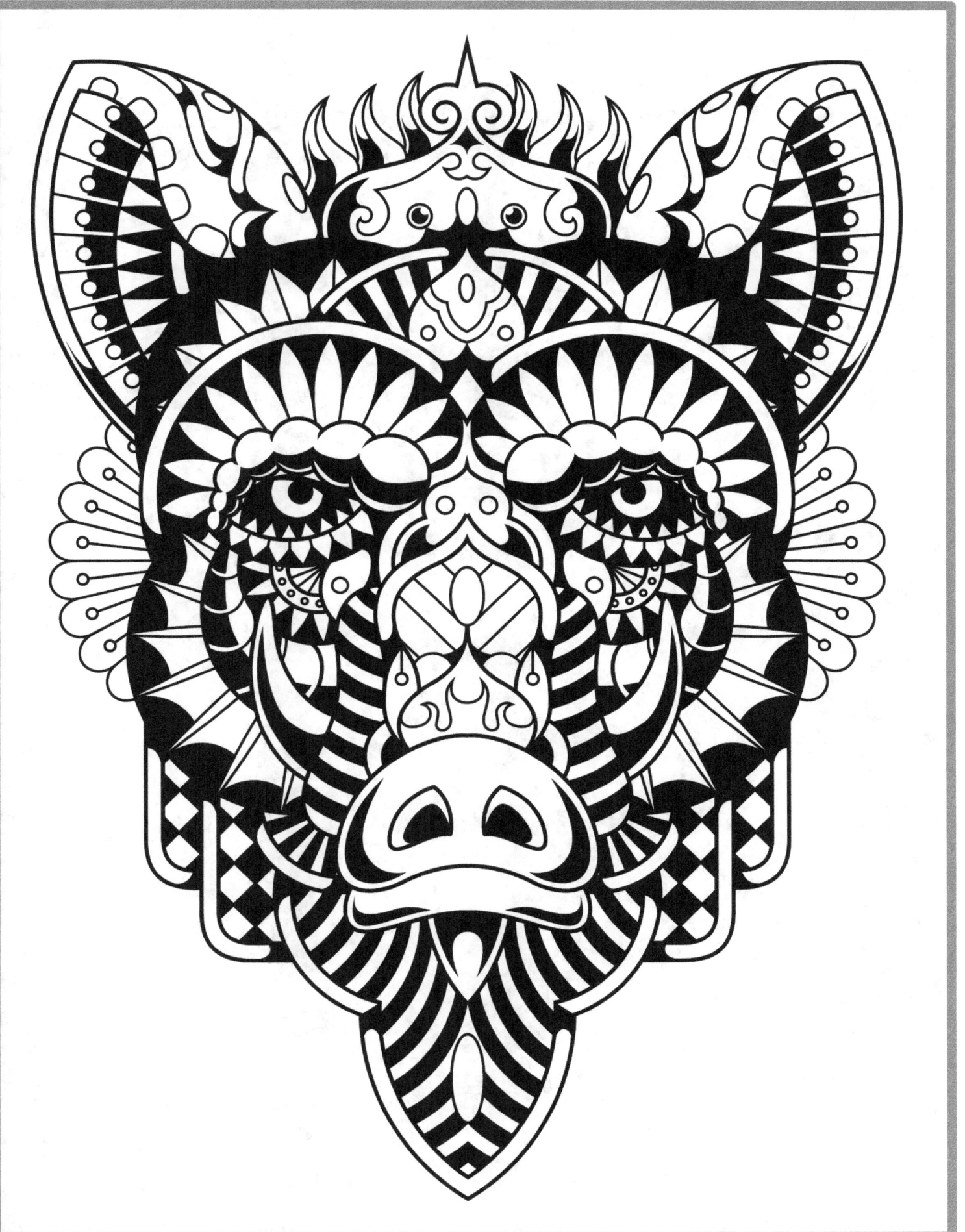

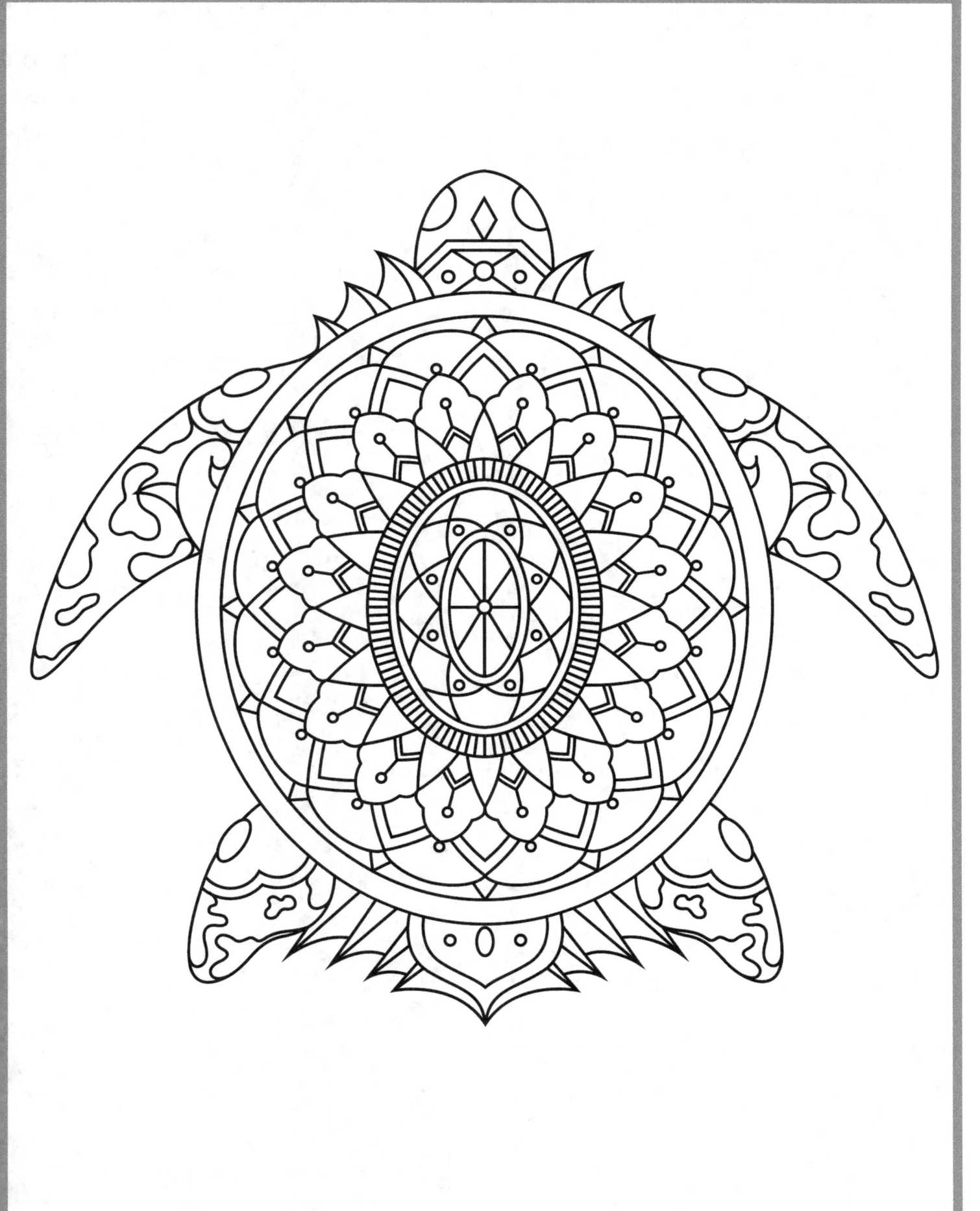

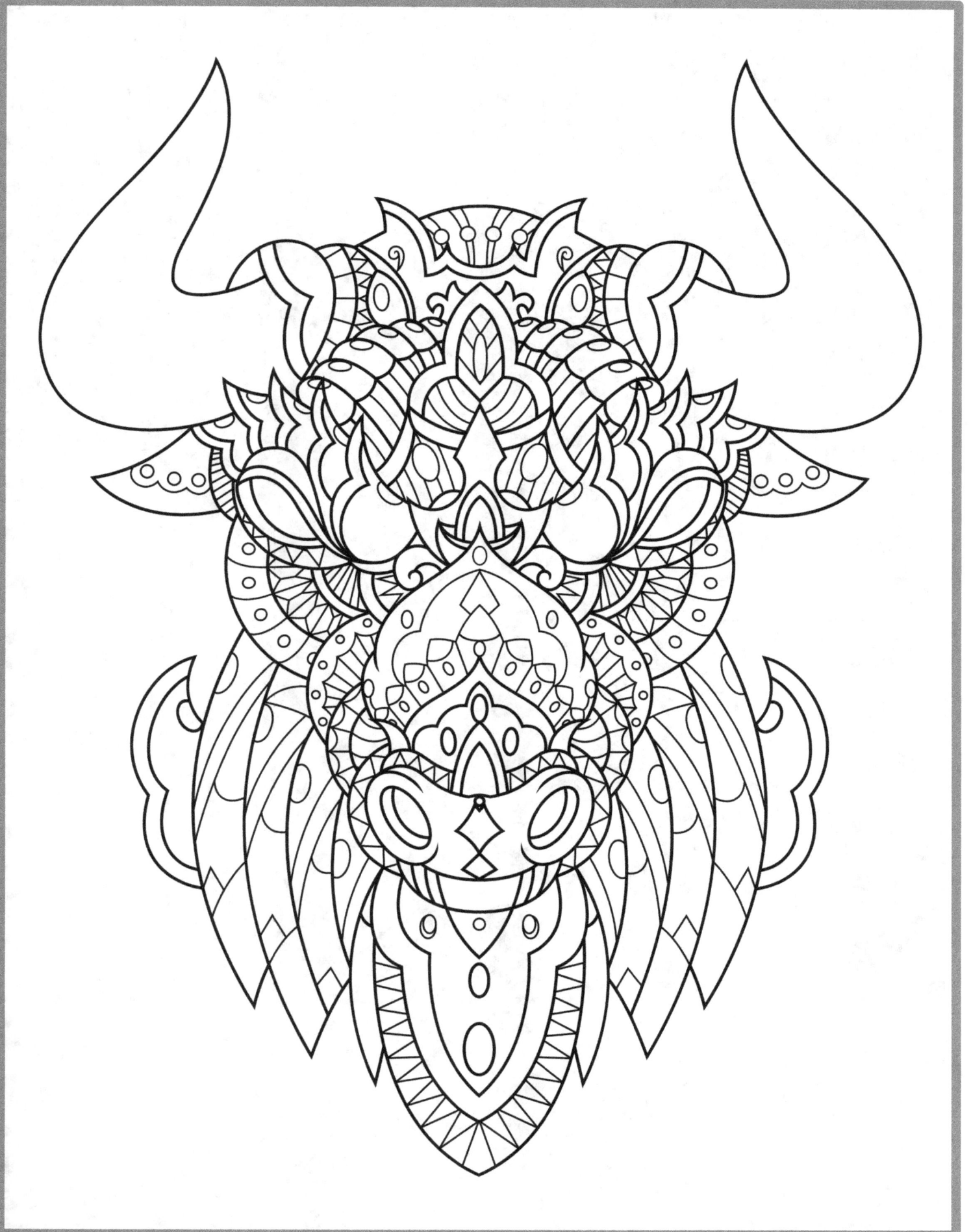

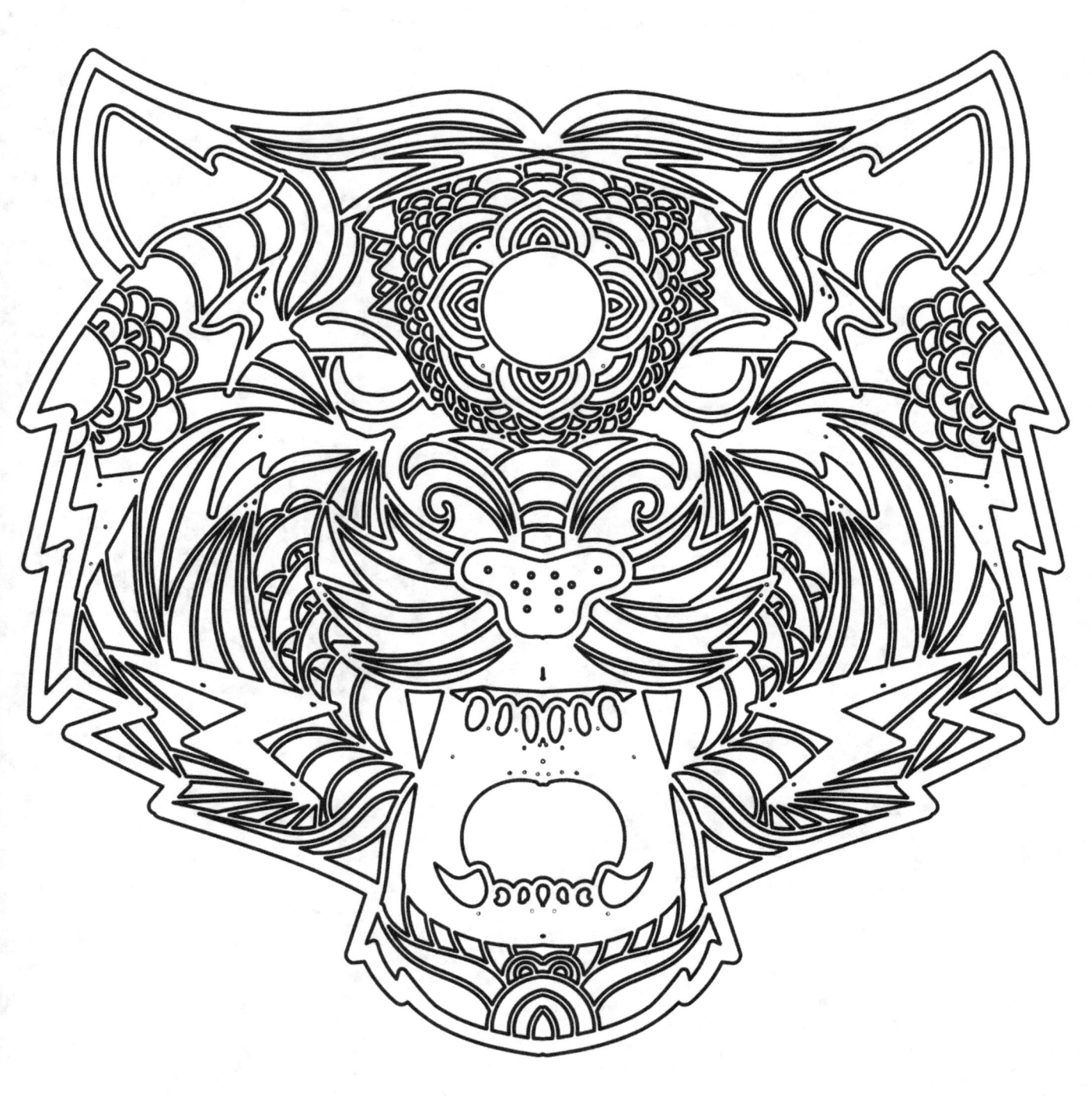

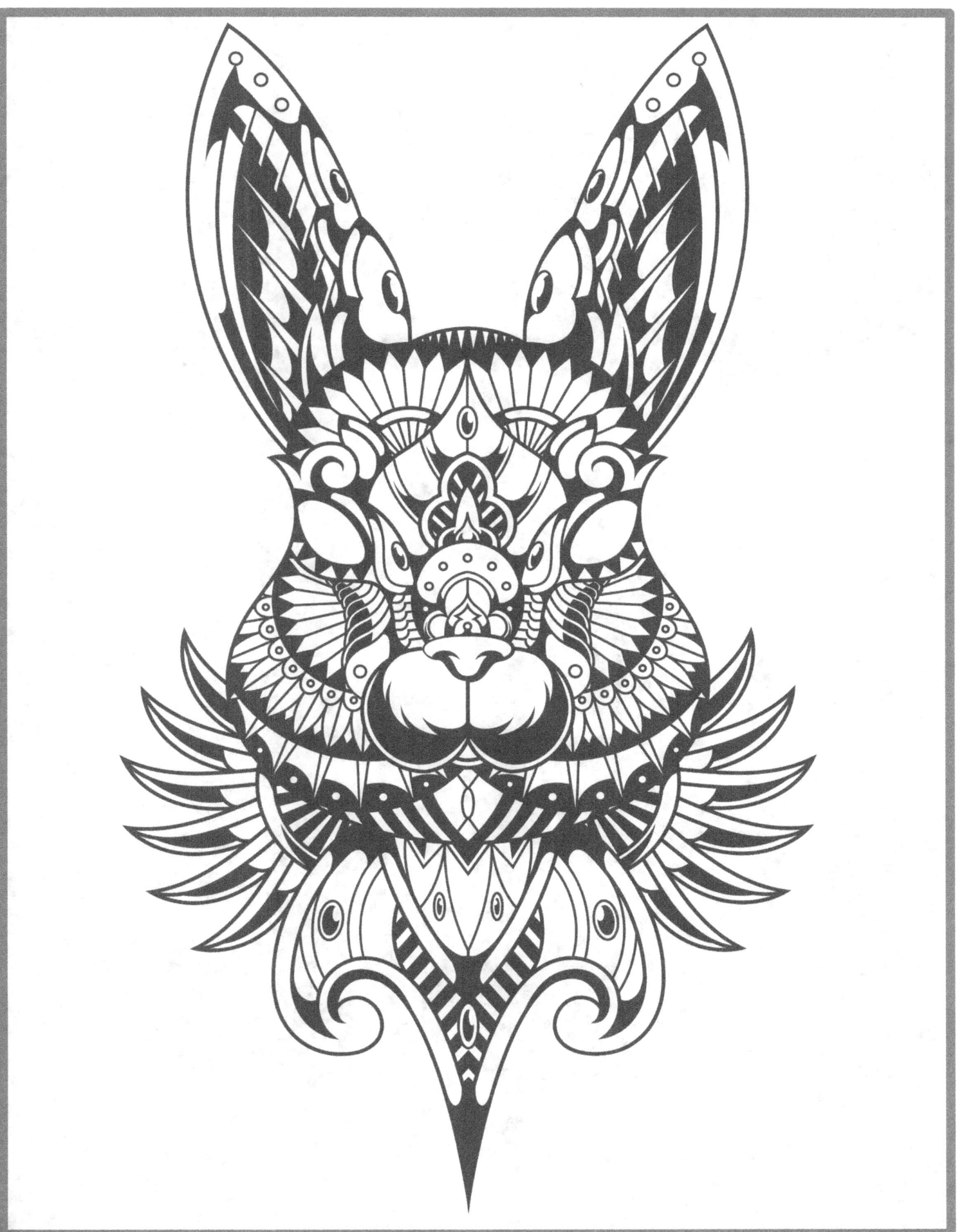

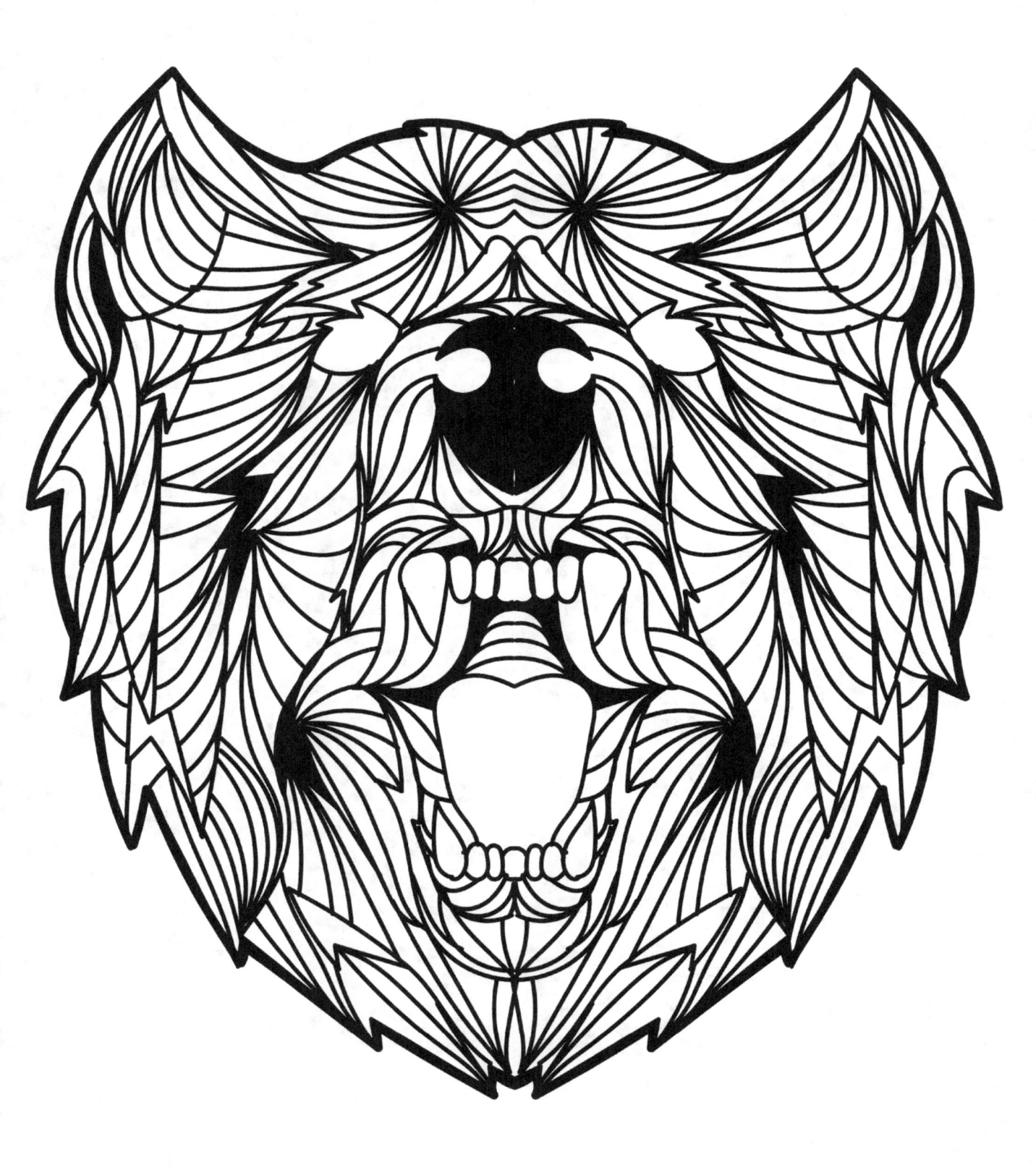

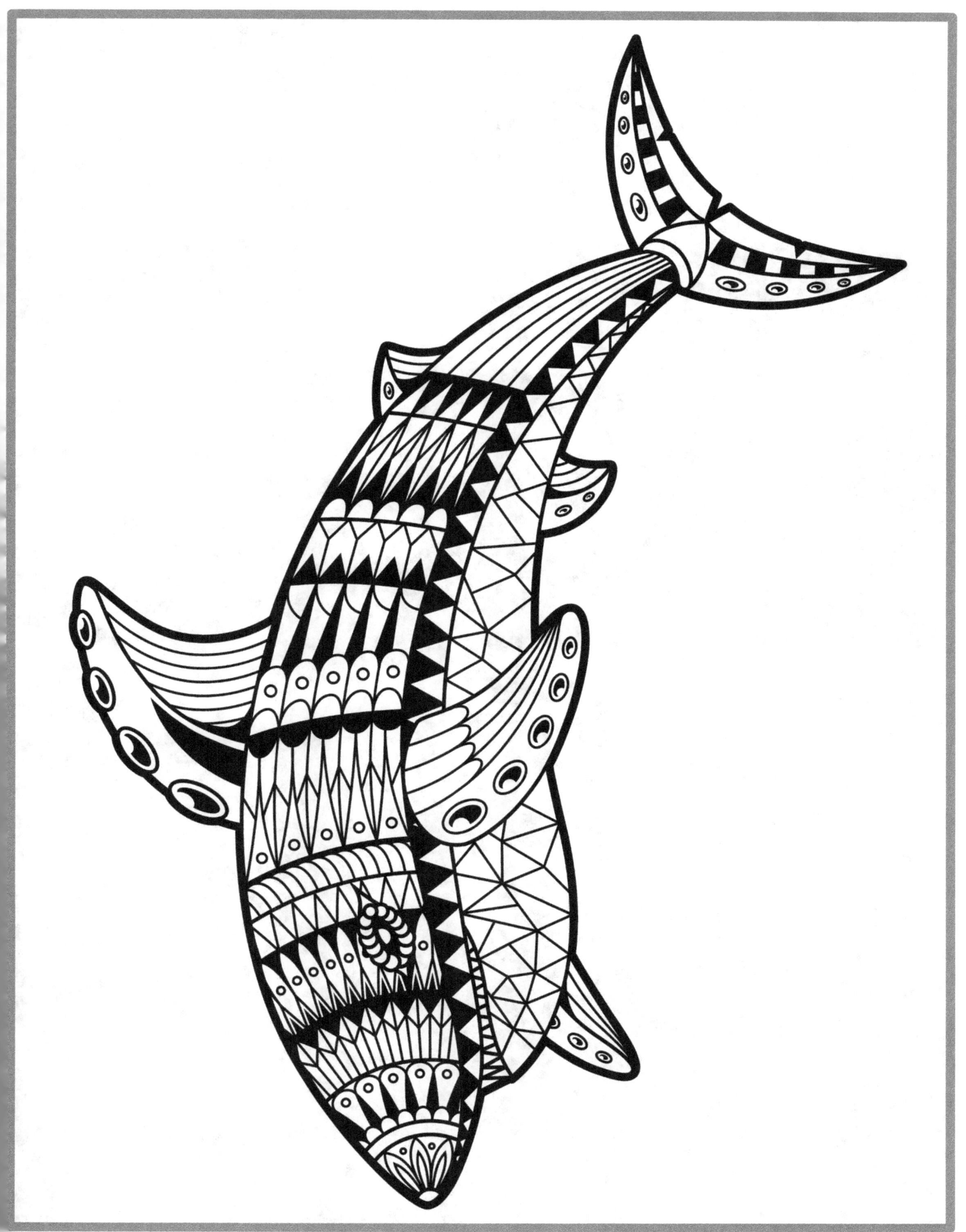

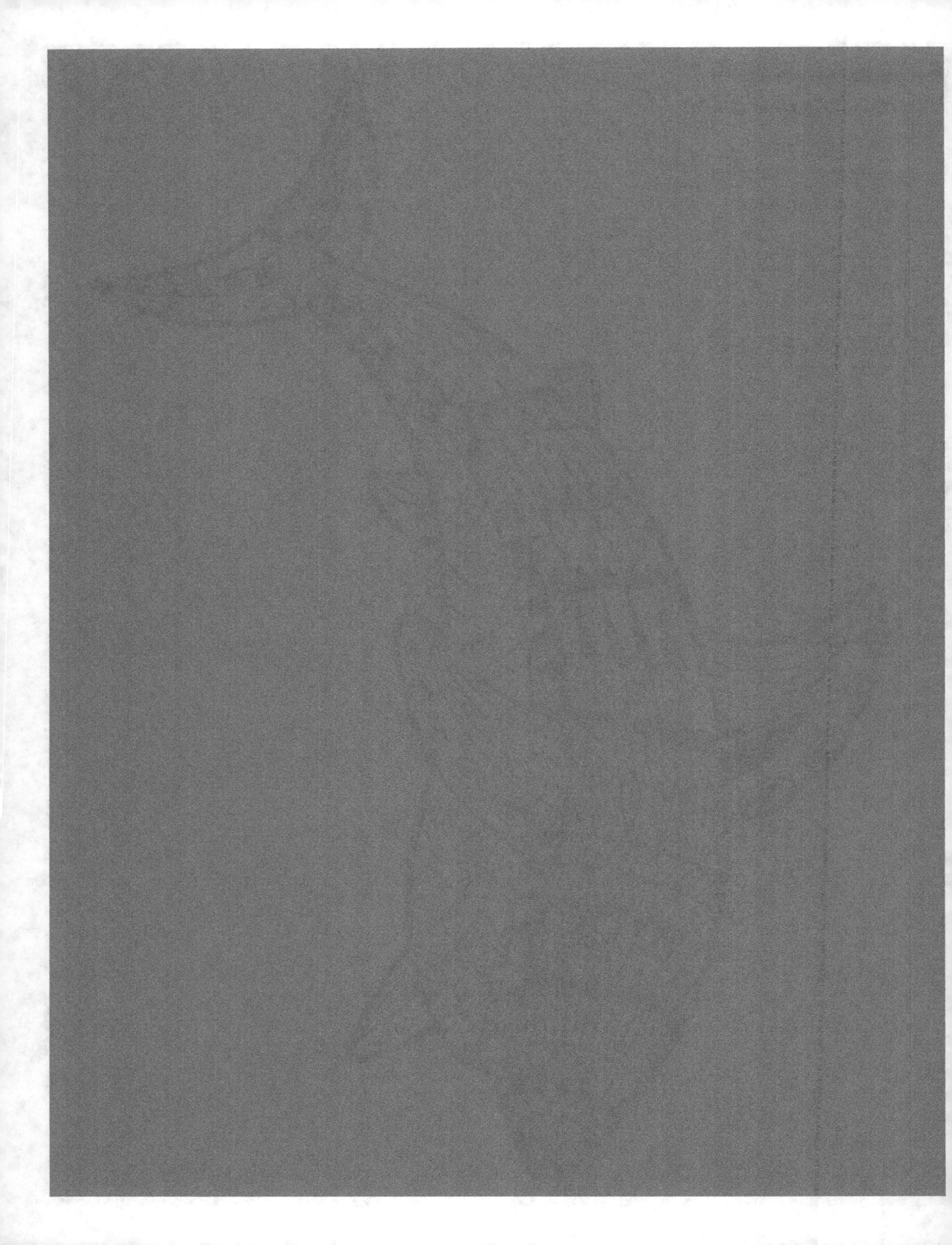

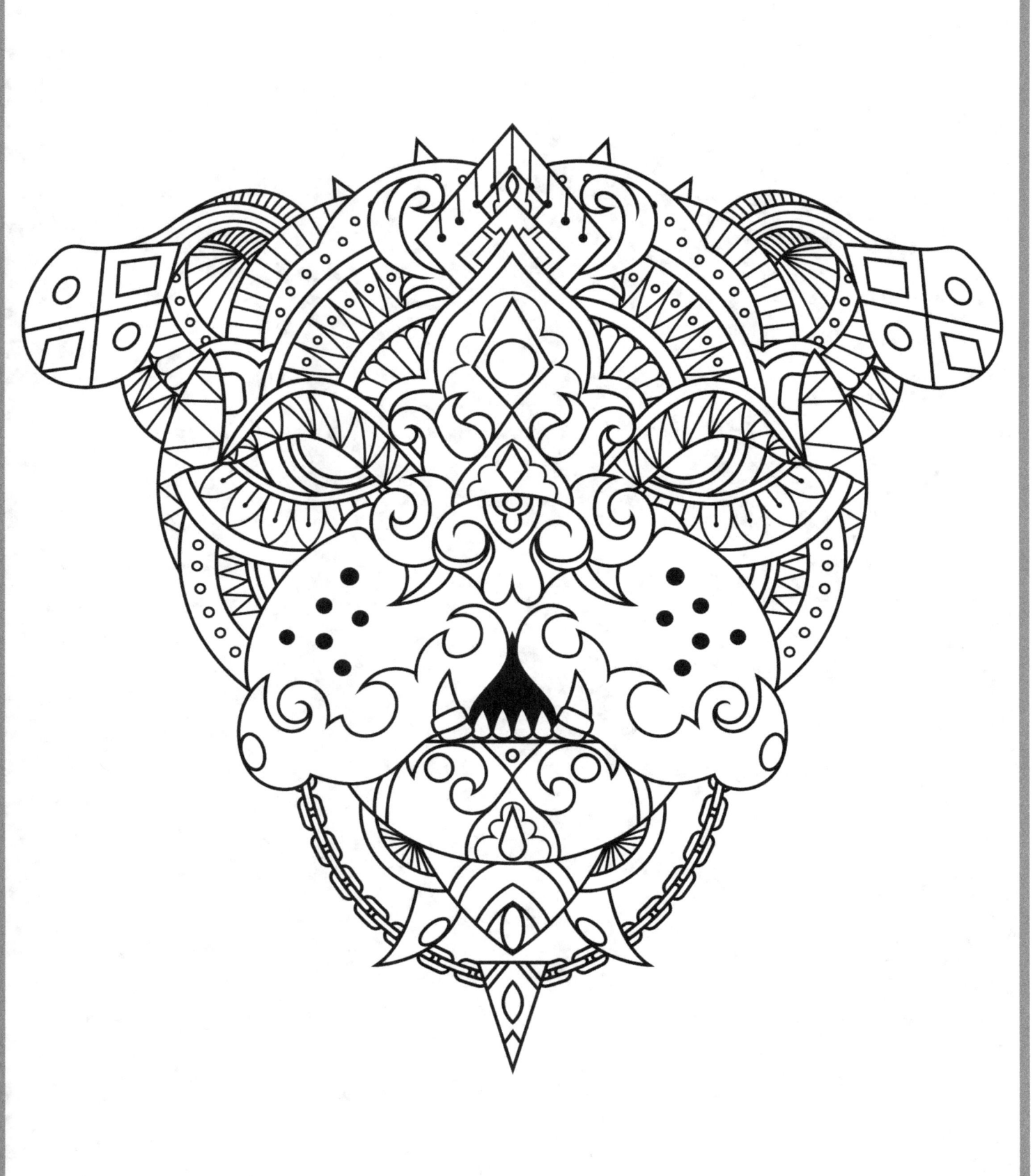

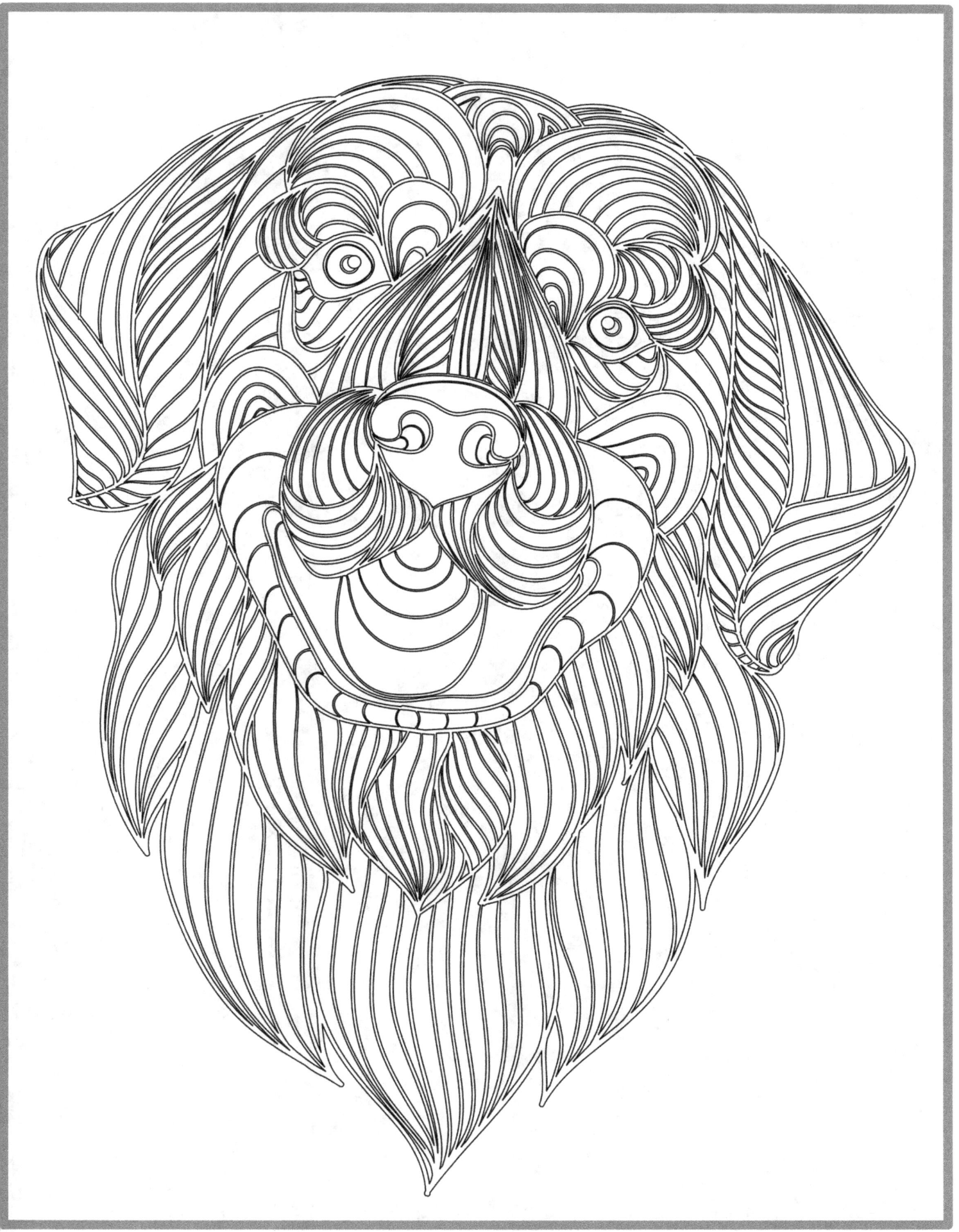

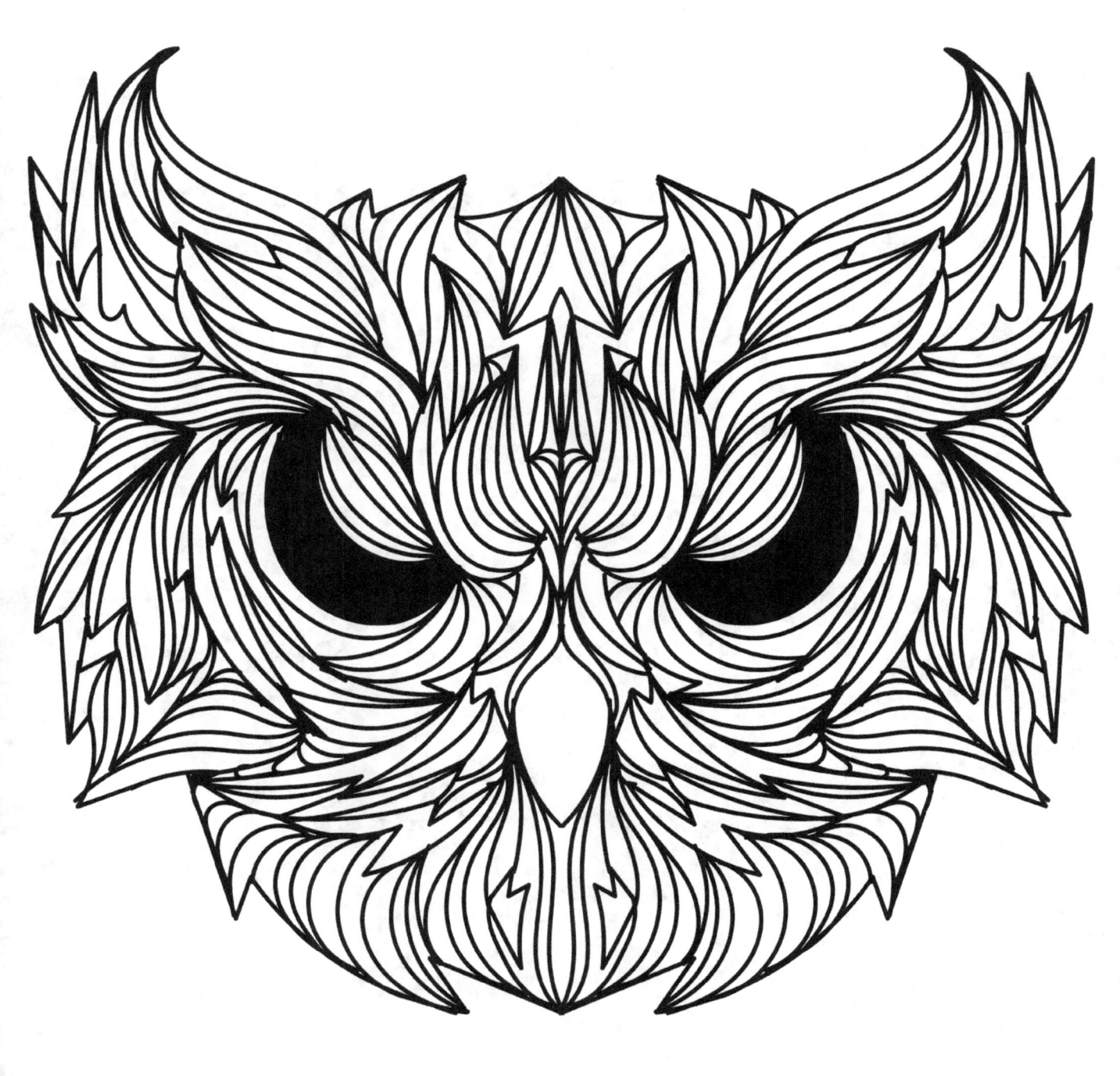

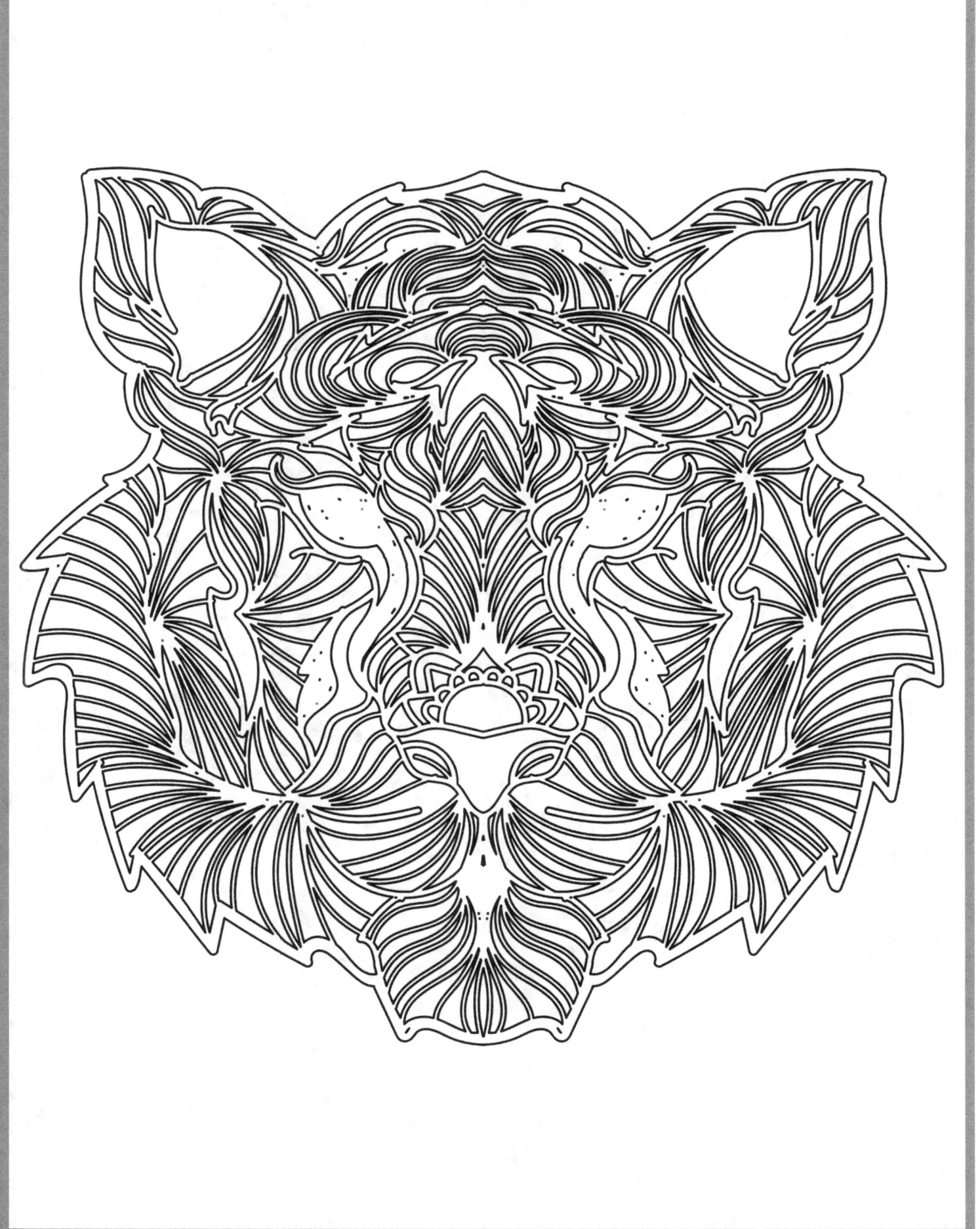

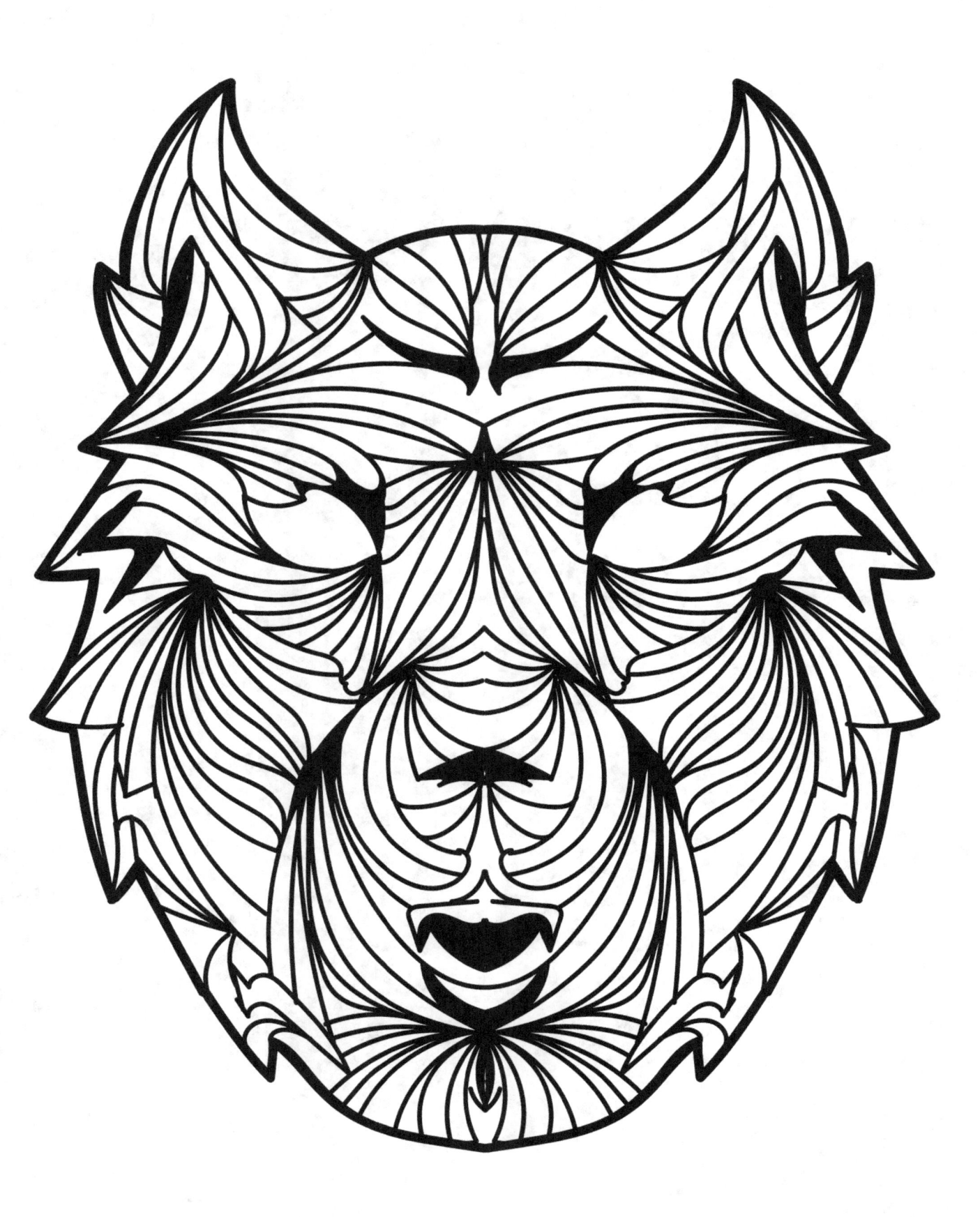

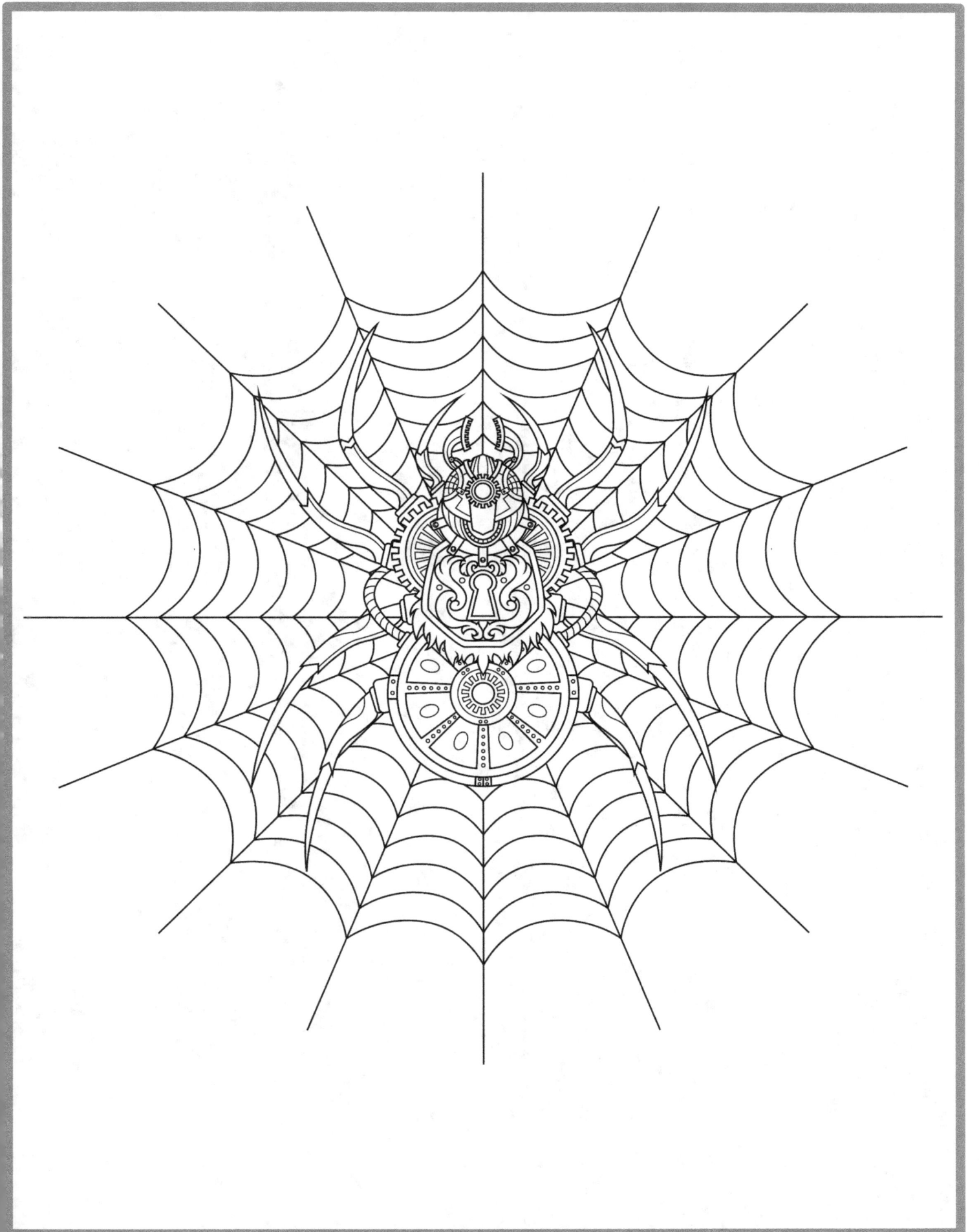

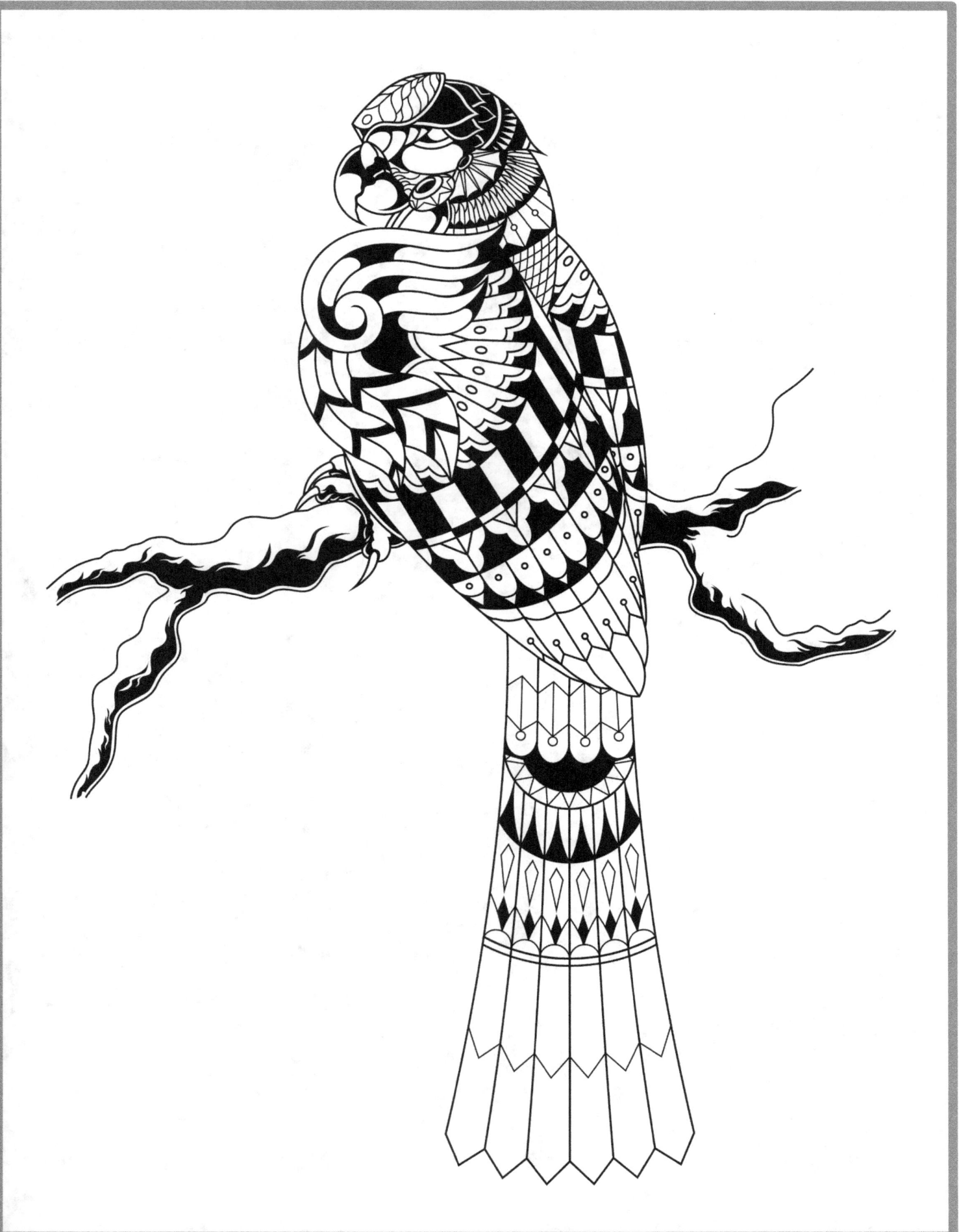

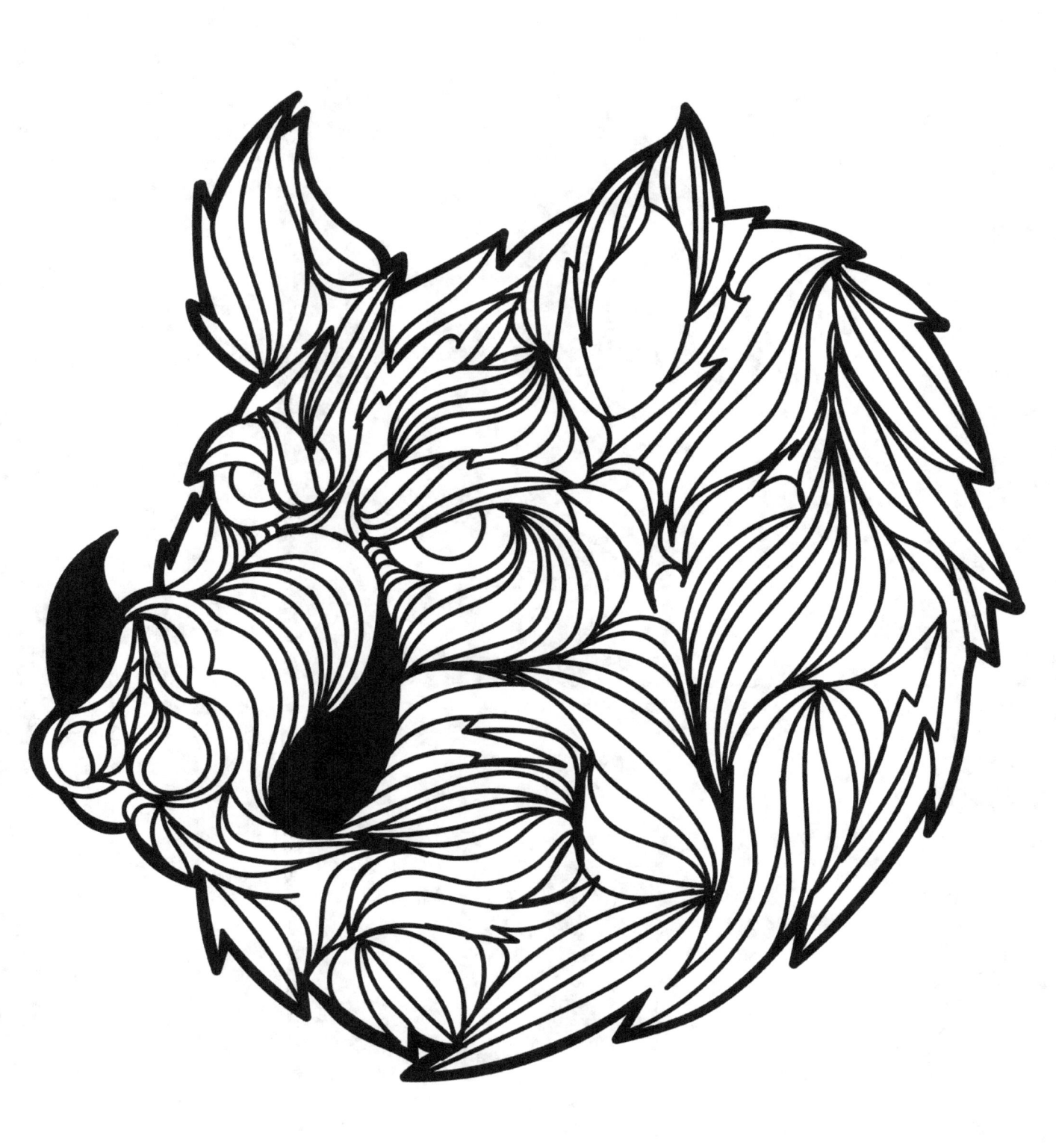

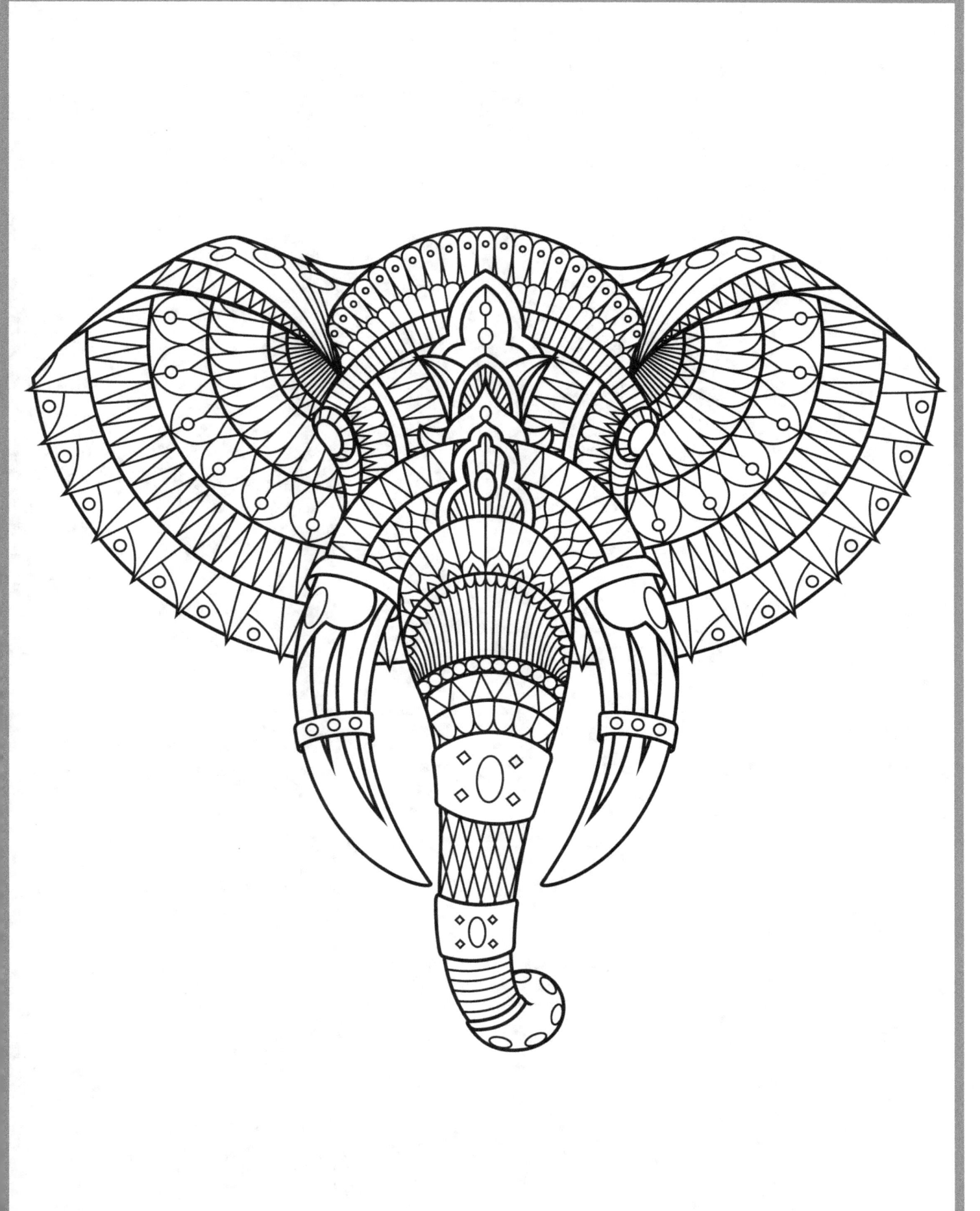

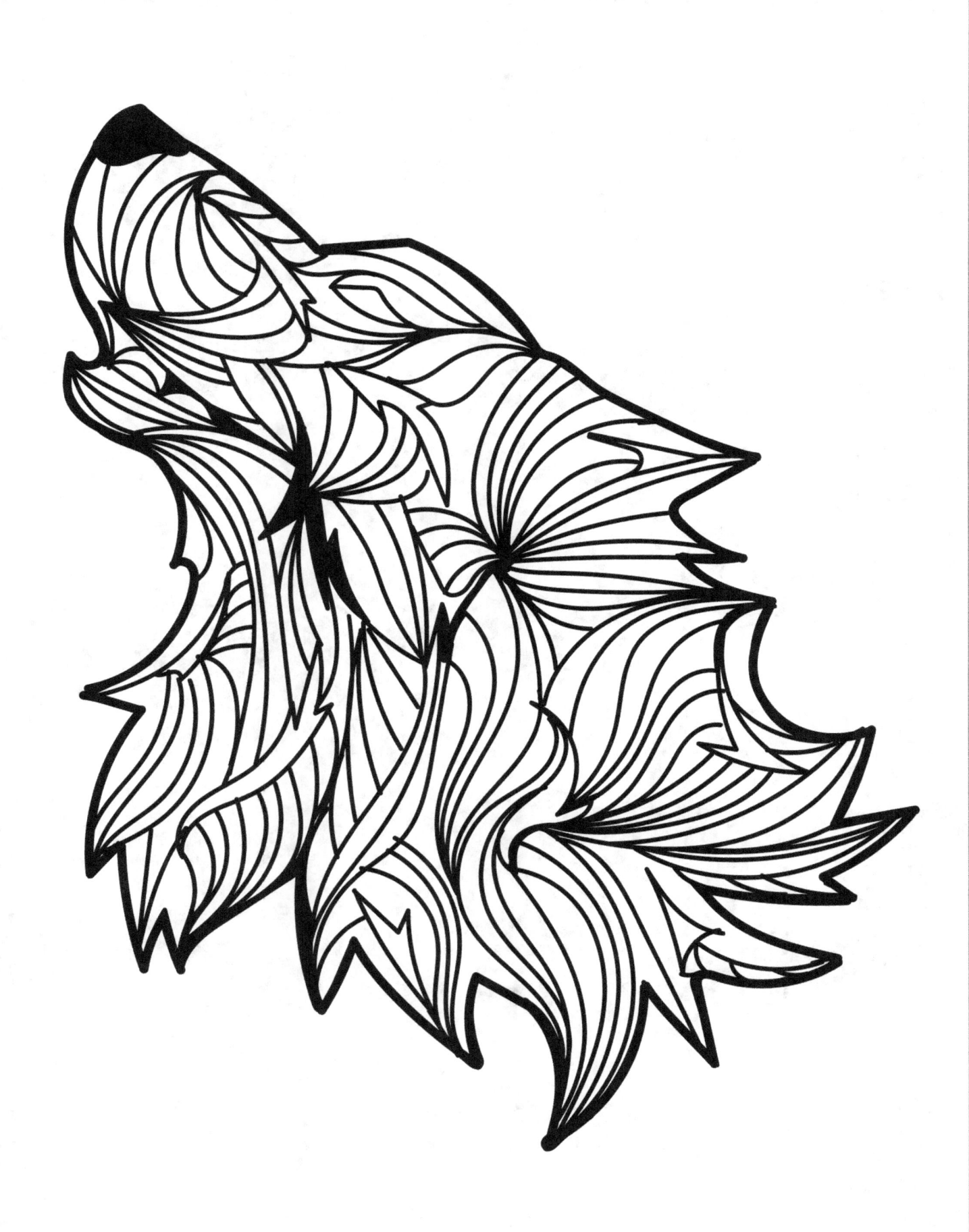

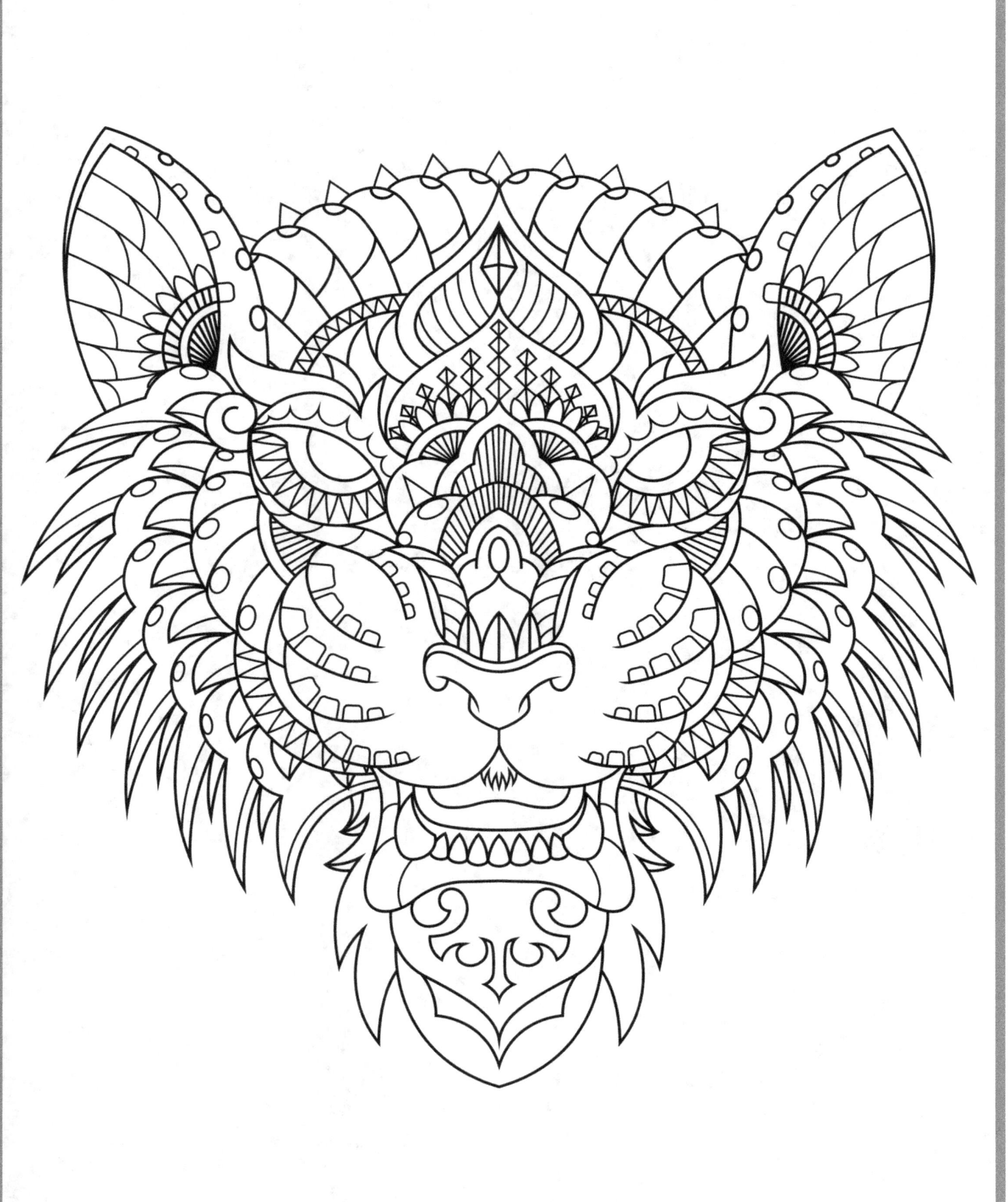

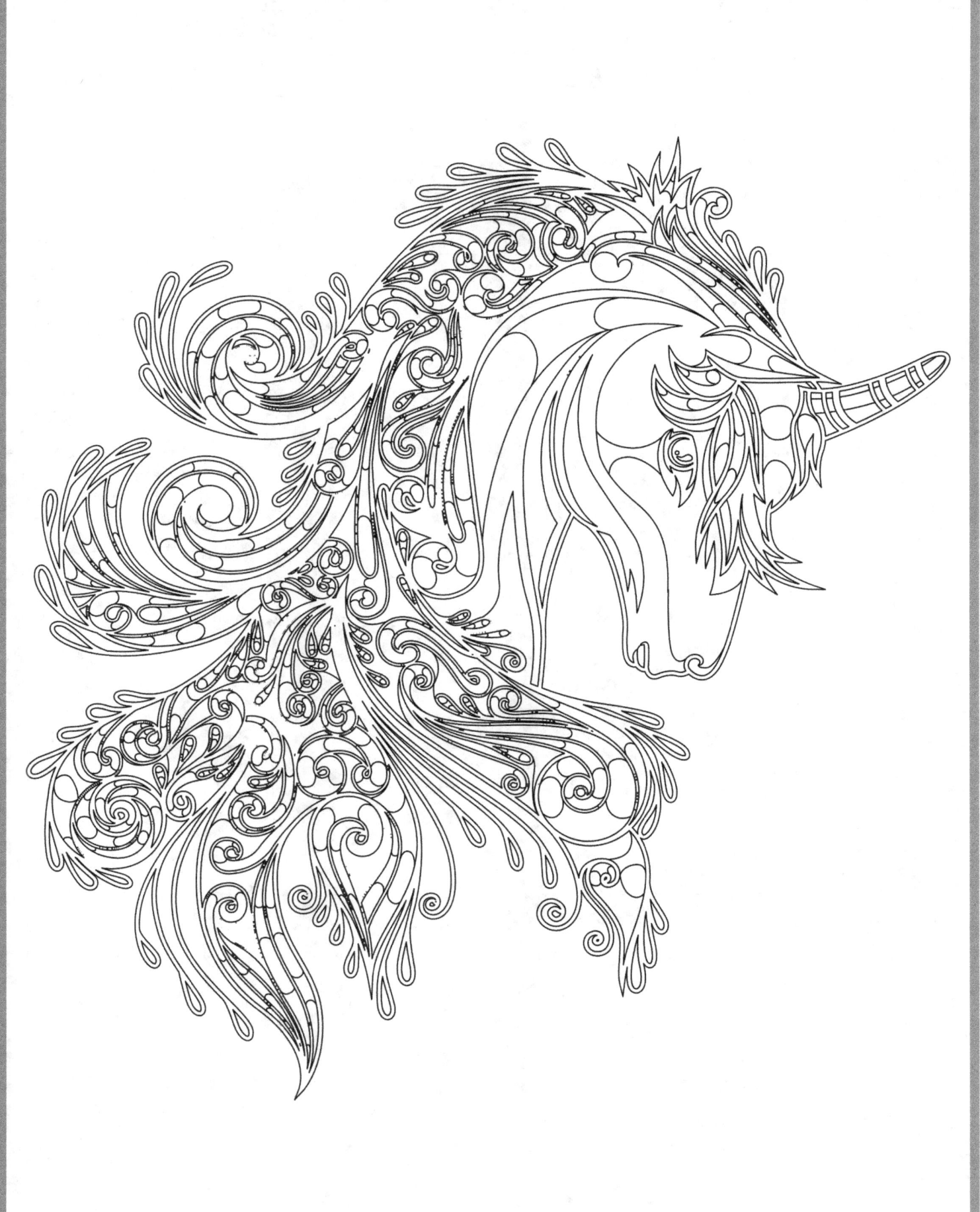

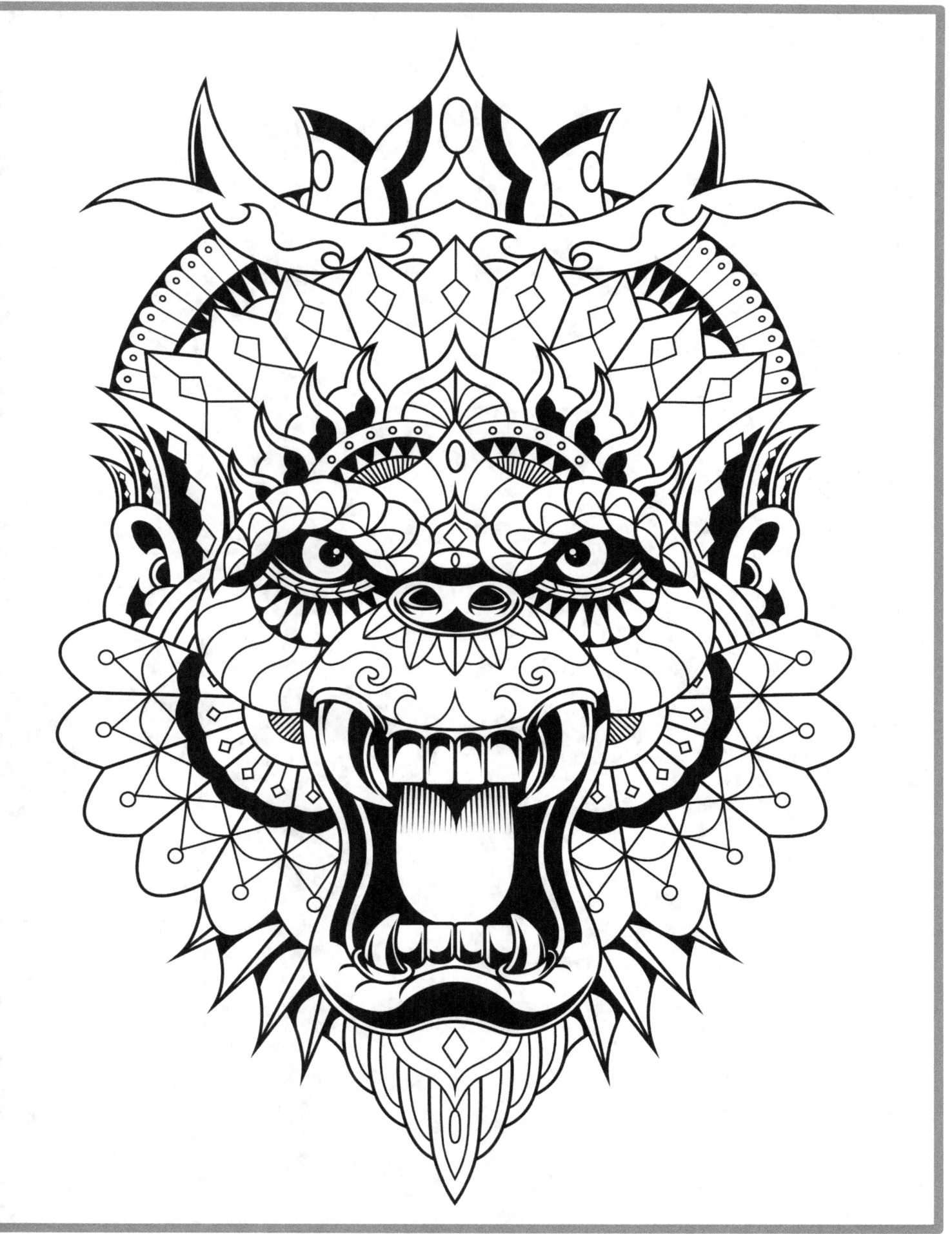

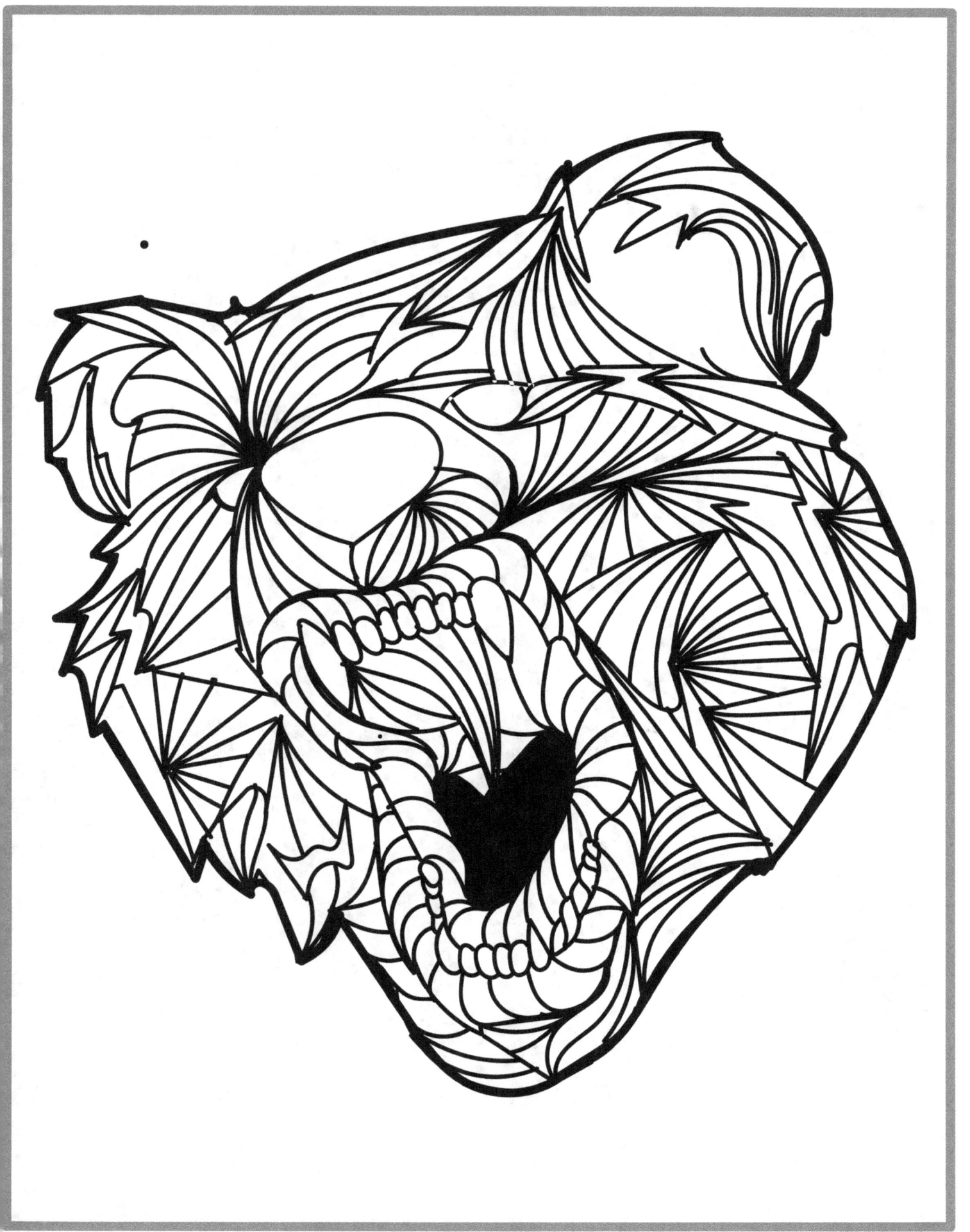

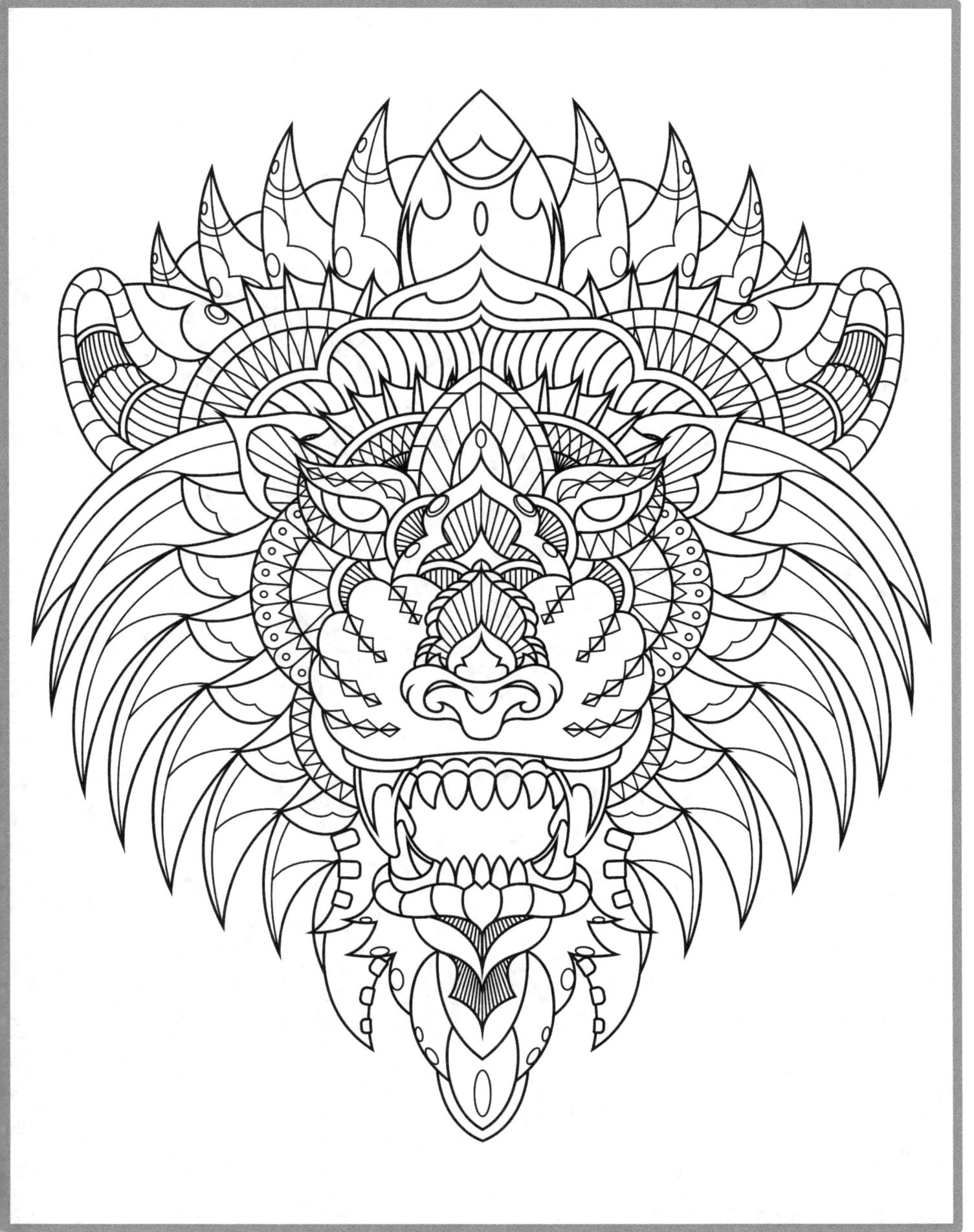

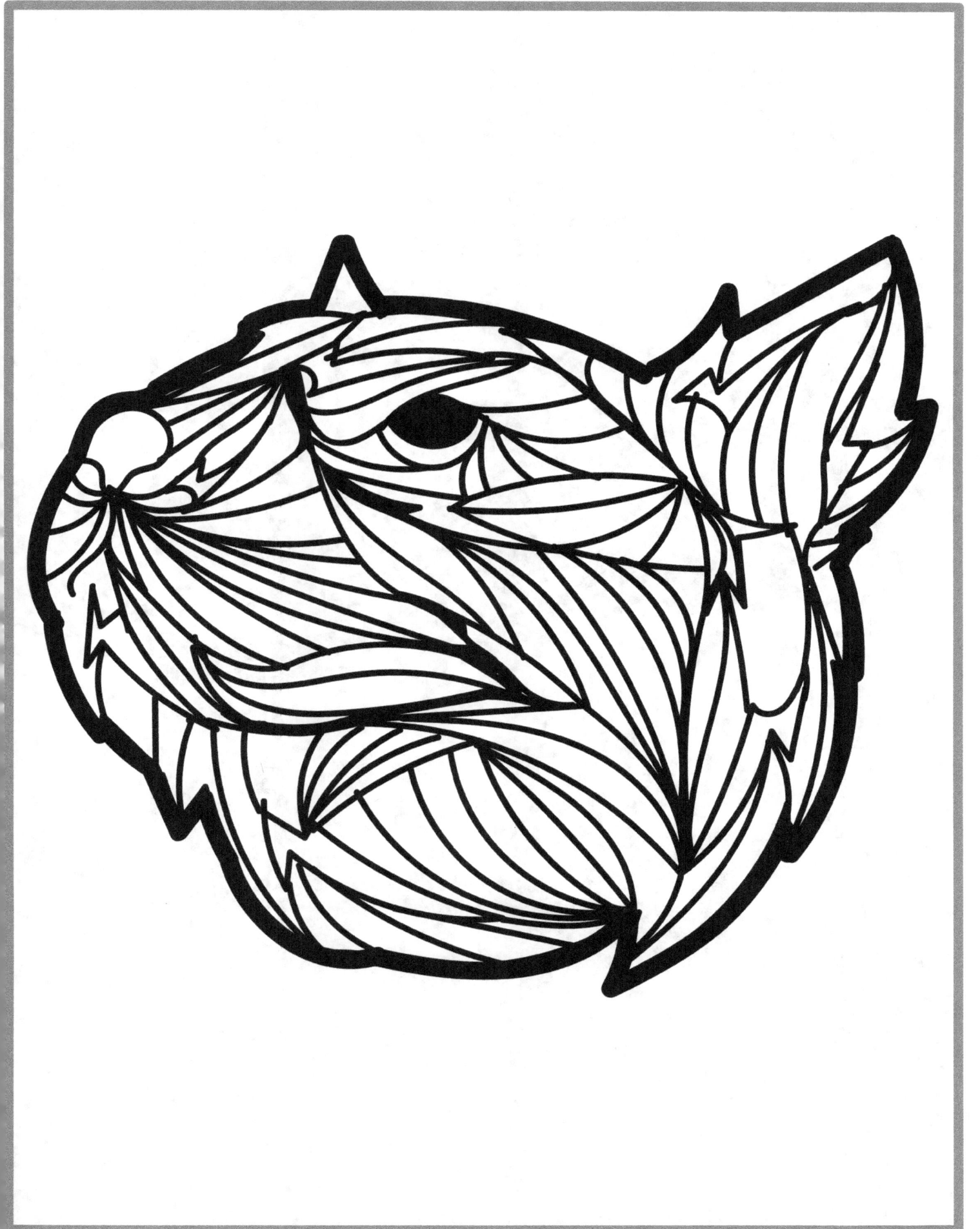

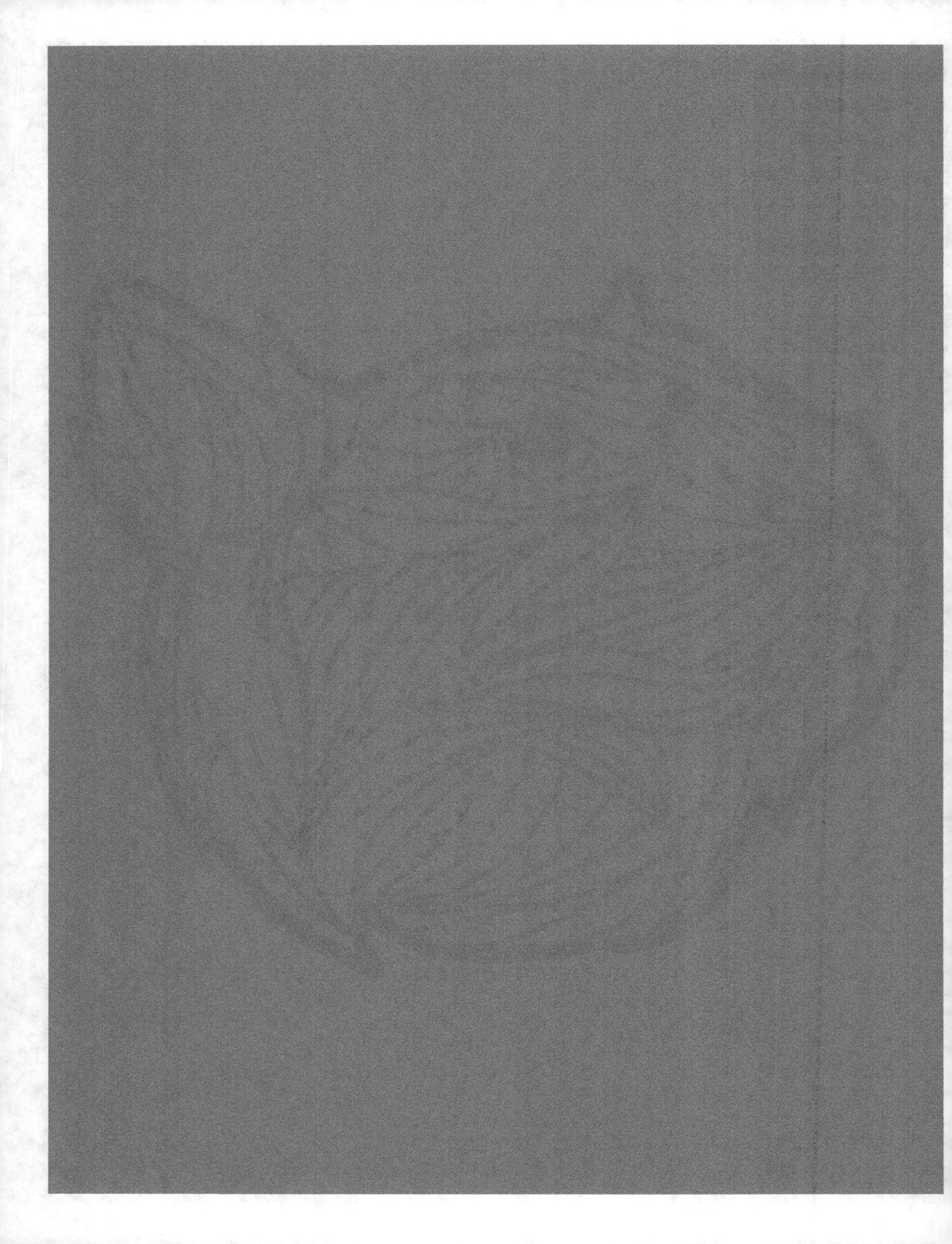

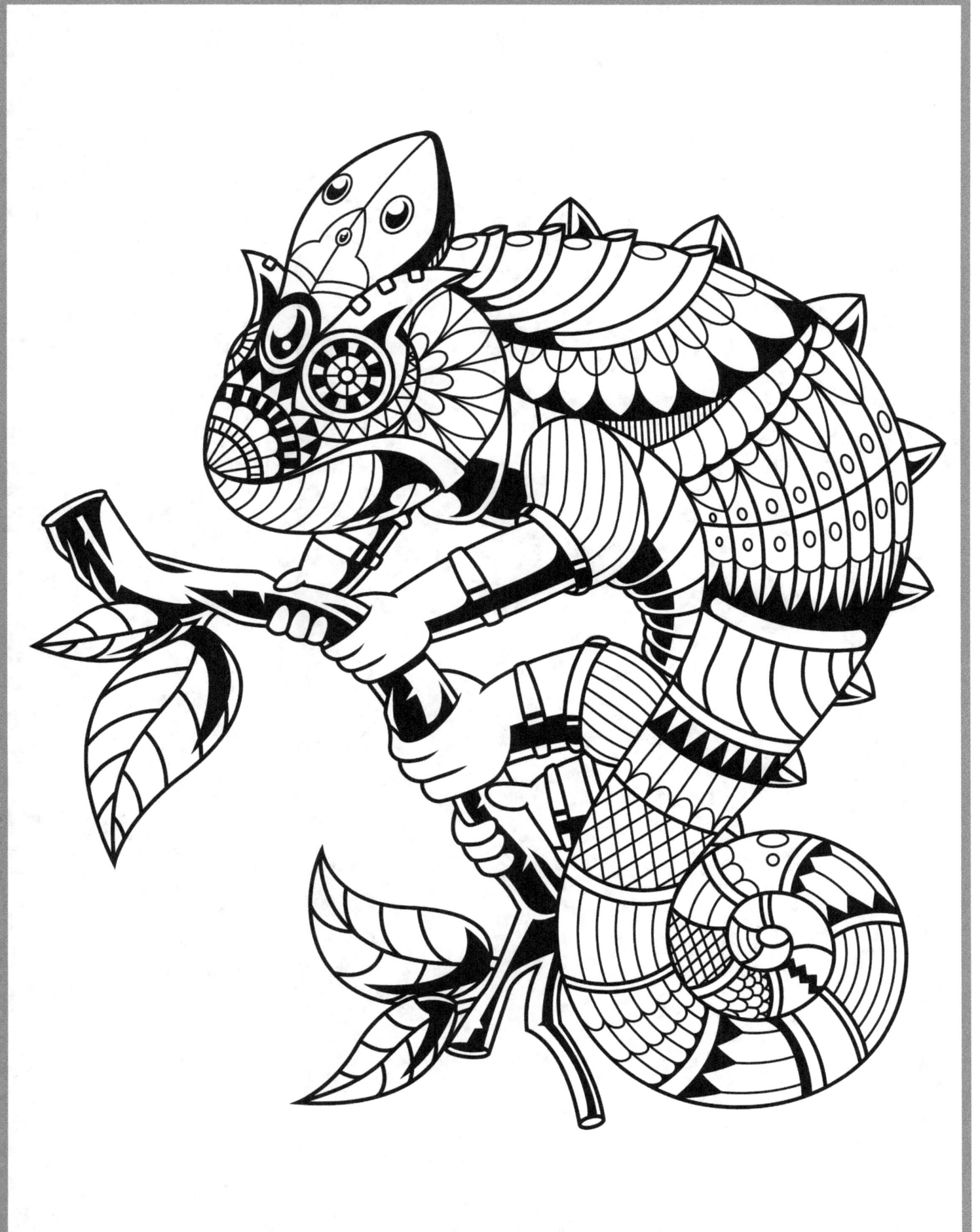

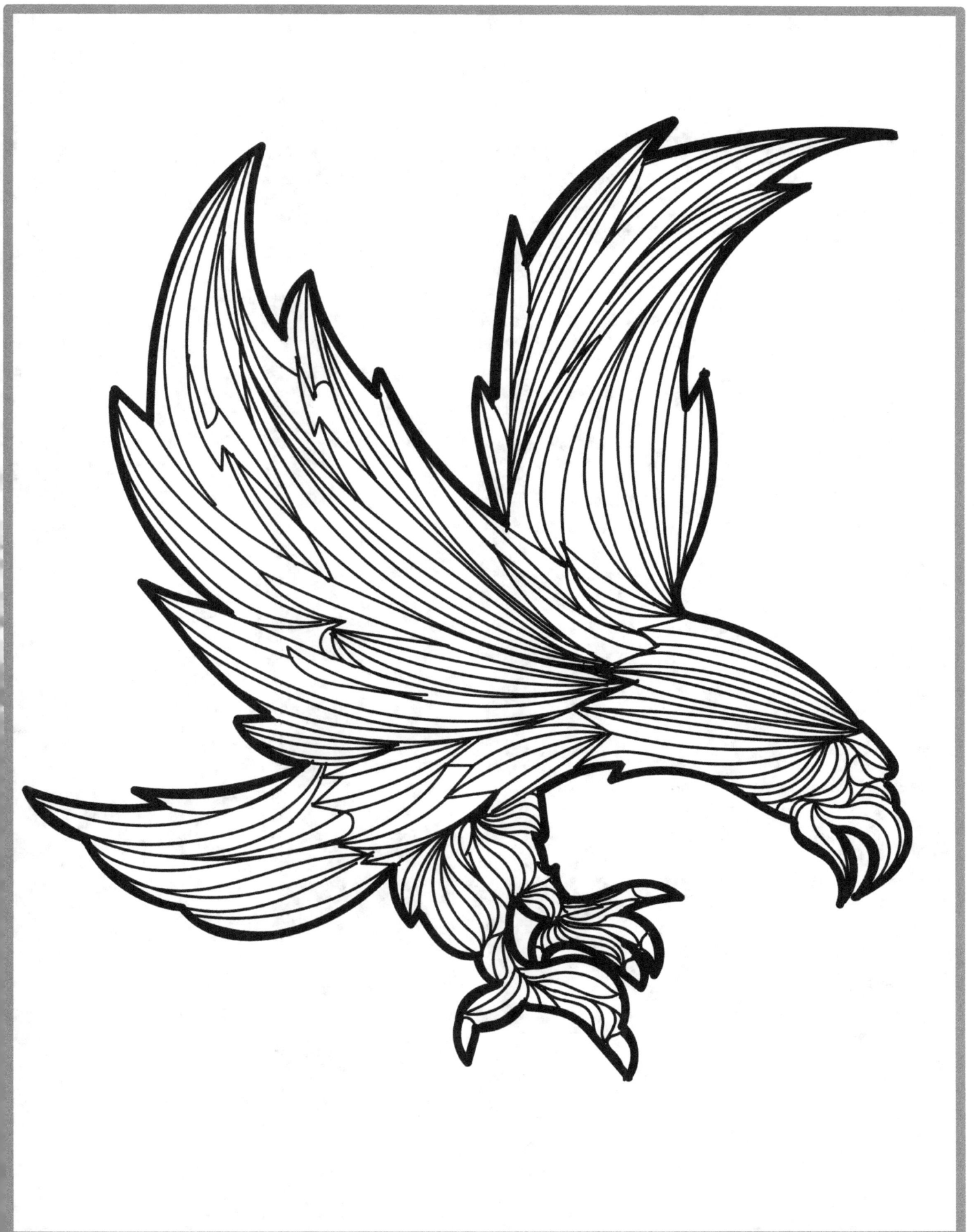

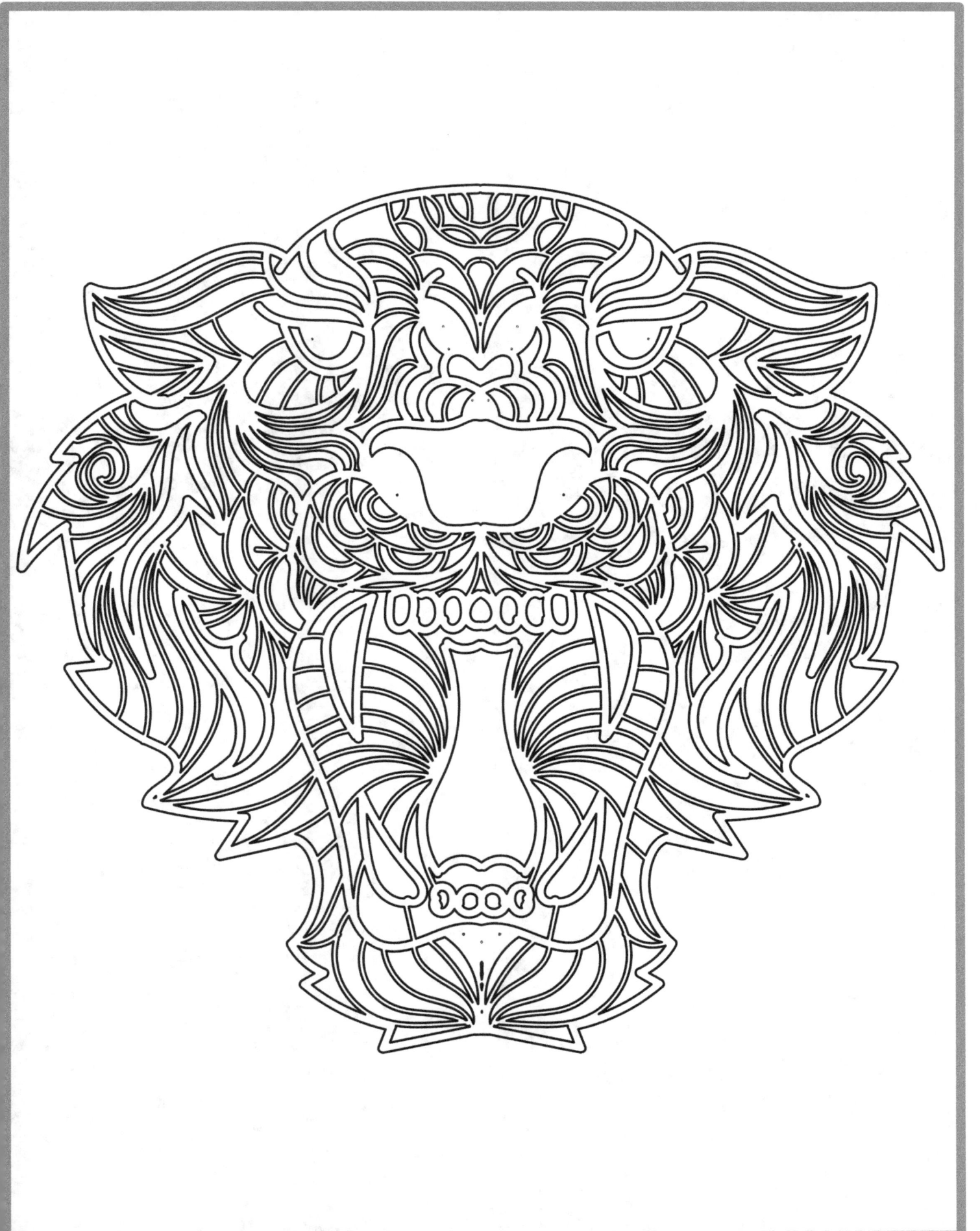

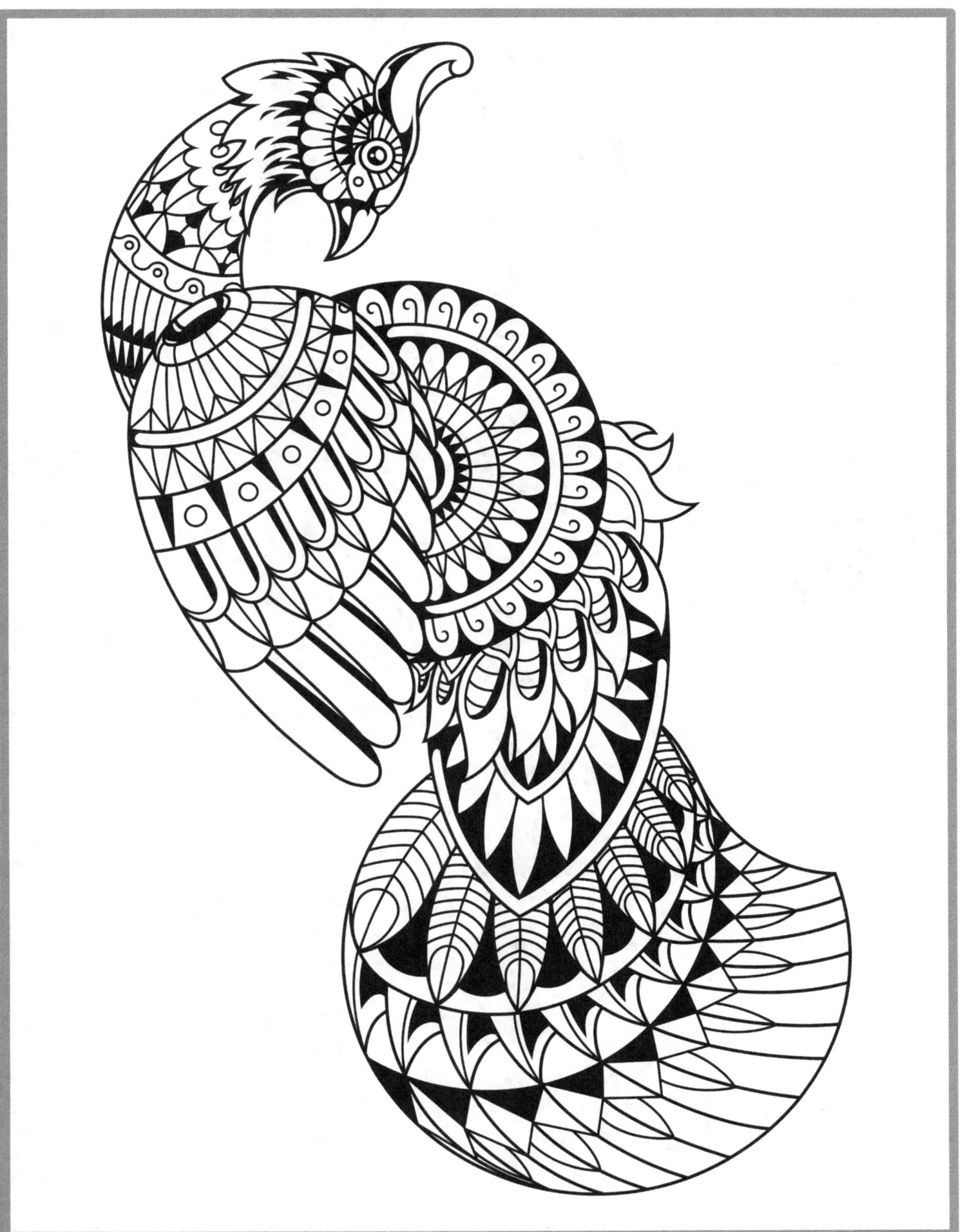

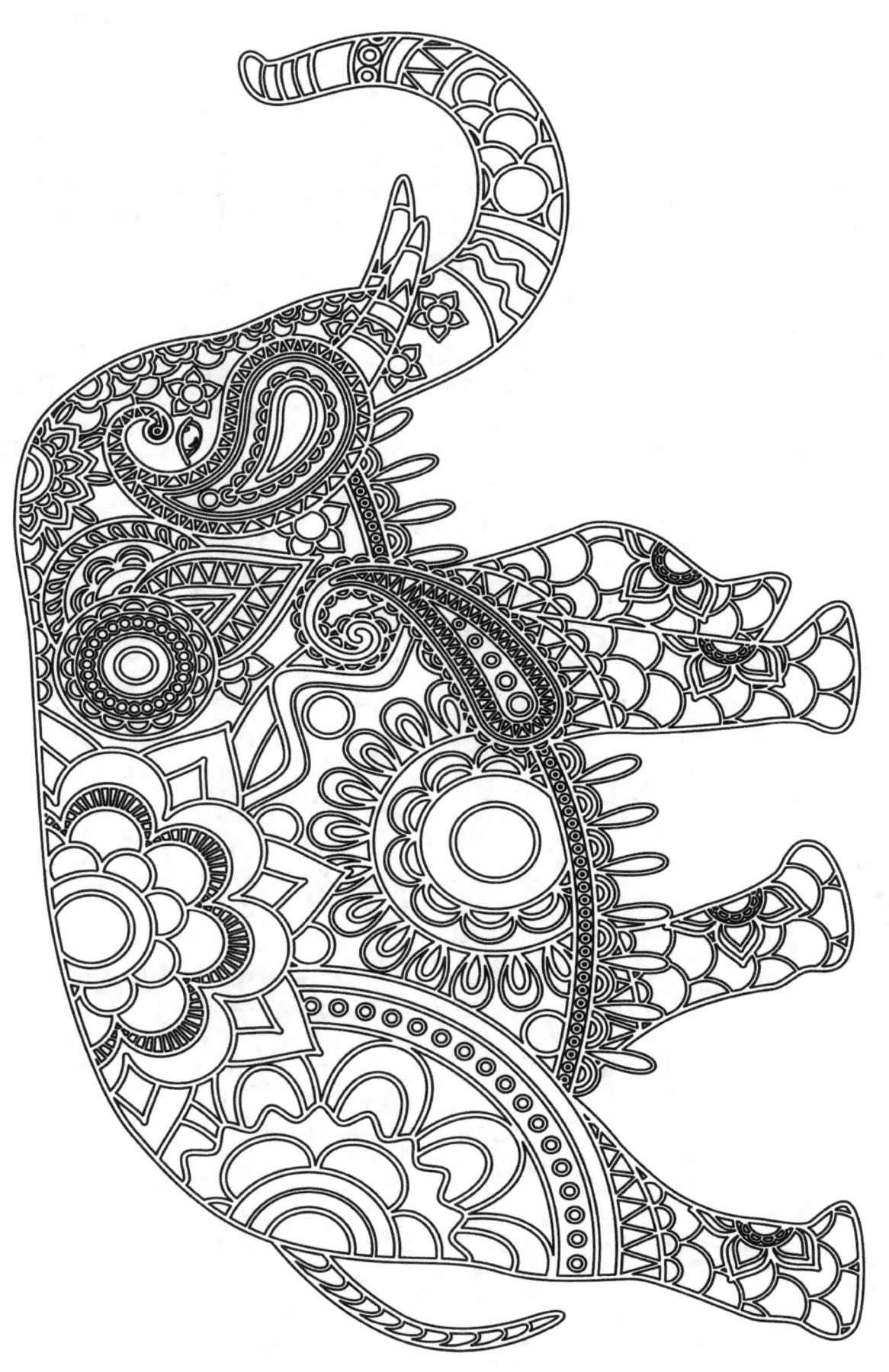

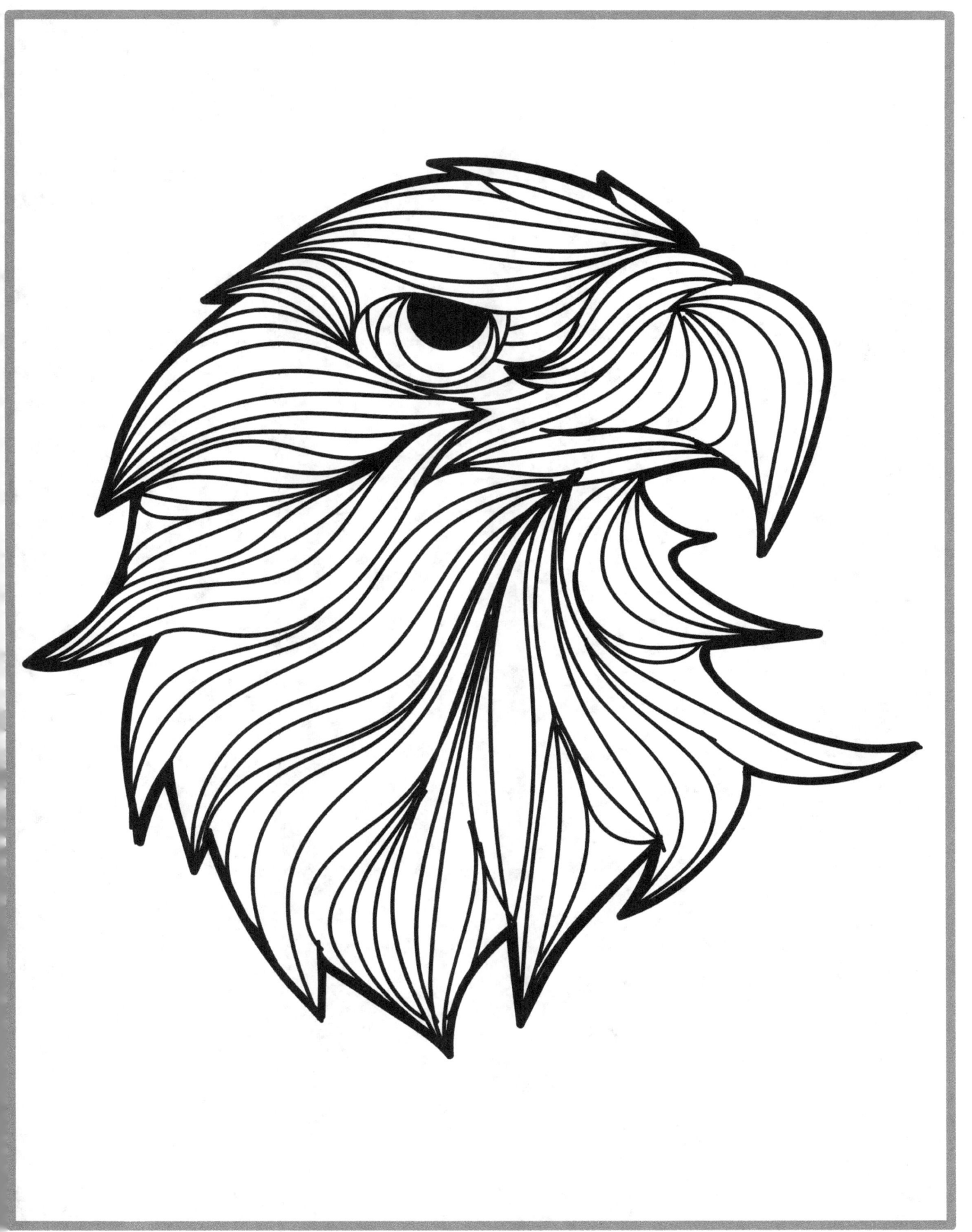

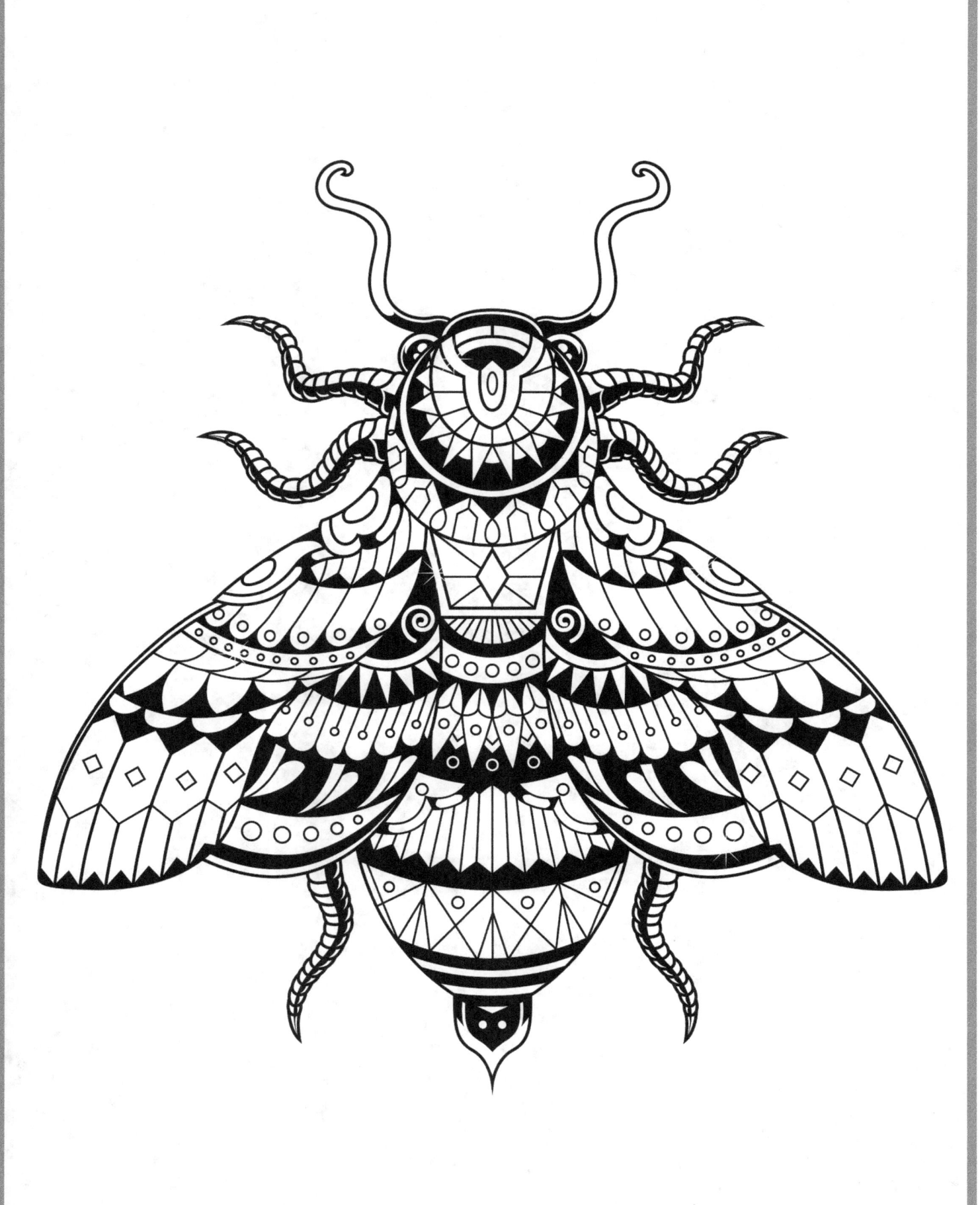

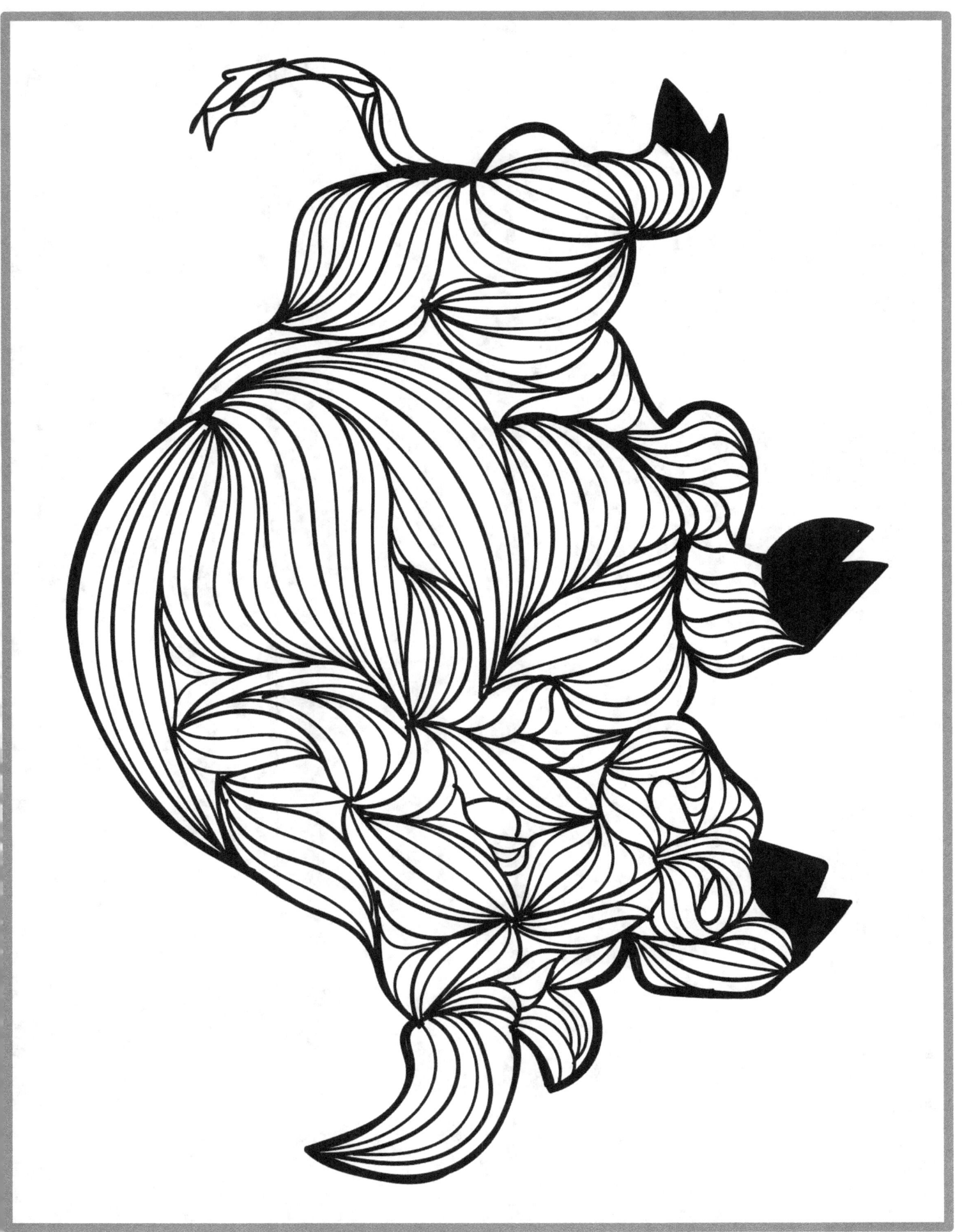

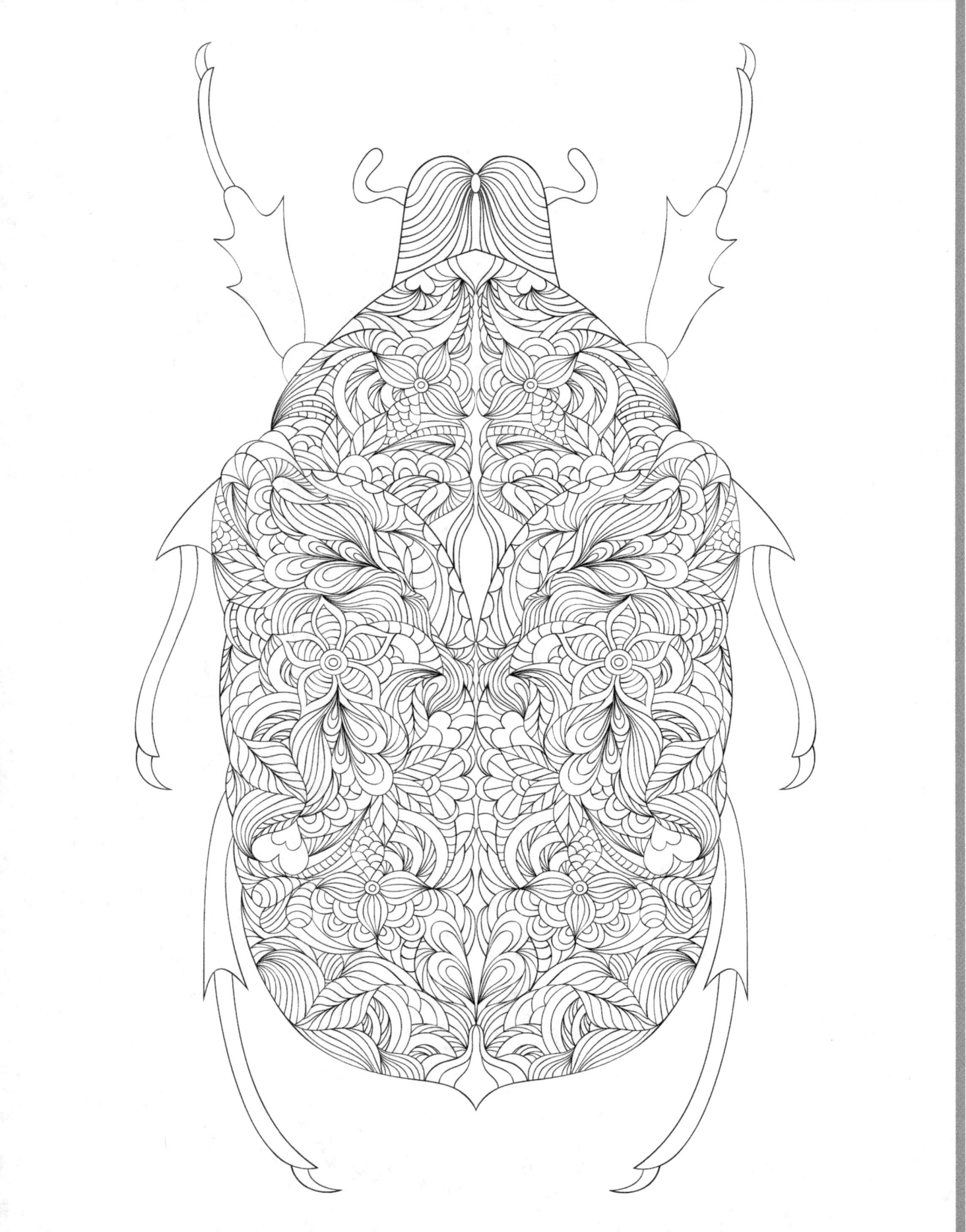

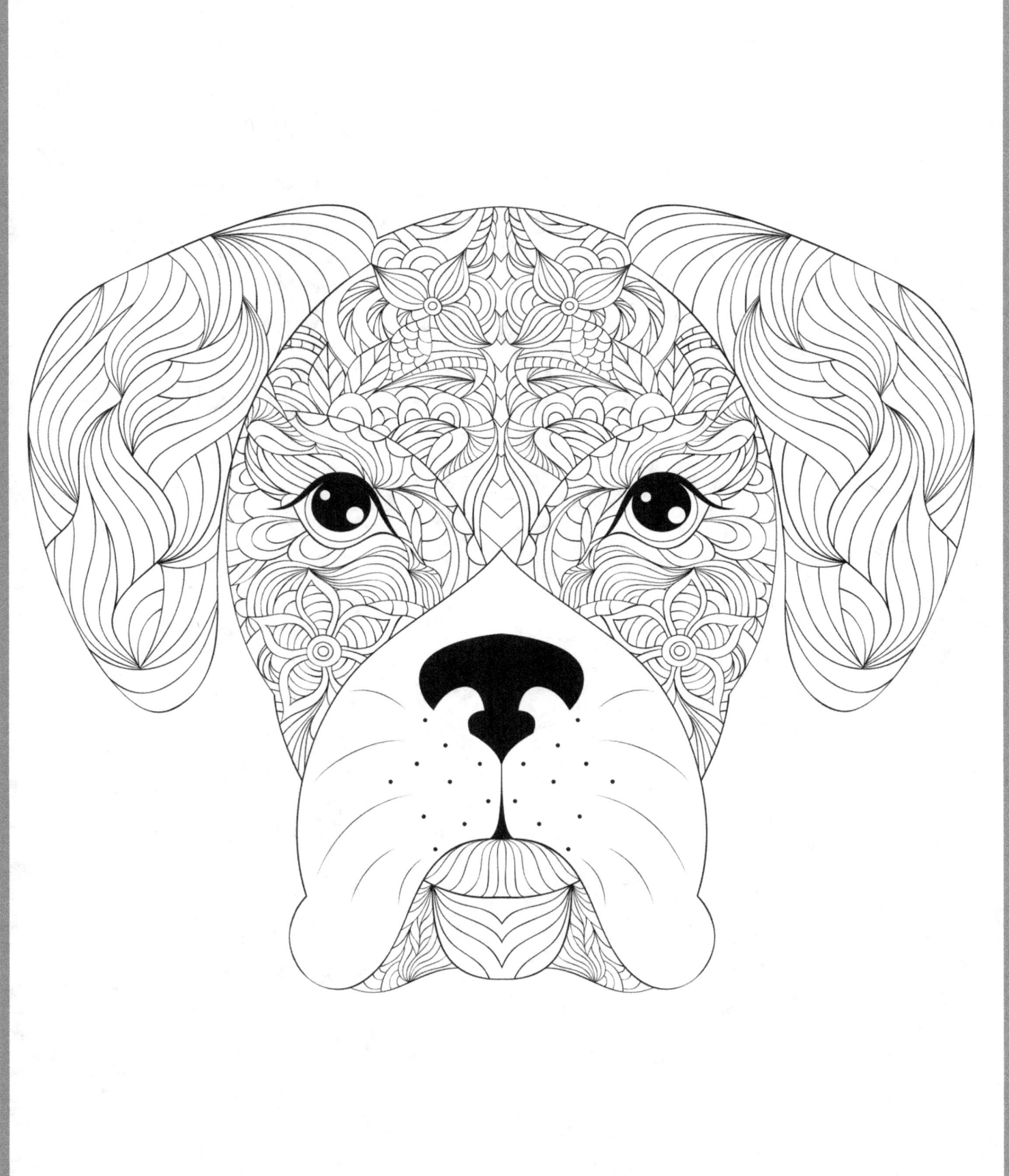